RUDOLF HENRY COLE VERNER.

THE BATTLE CRUISERS

AT THE

ACTION OF THE FALKLAND ISLANDS

BY

COMMANDER RUDOLF VERNER, ROYAL NAVY,

H.M.S. INFLEXIBLE

EDITED BY COLONEL WILLOUGHBY VERNER

WITH

A MEMOIR OF THE AUTHOR

BY HAROLD HODGE

The Naval & Military Press Ltd

Published by

The Naval & Military Press Ltd
Unit 5 Riverside, Brambleside
Bellbrook Industrial Estate
Uckfield, East Sussex
TN22 1QQ England

Tel: +44 (0)1825 749494

www.naval-military-press.com
www.nmarchive.com

In reprinting in facsimile from the original, any imperfections are inevitably reproduced and the quality may fall short of modern type and cartographic standards.

DEDICATED

BY PERMISSION

TO

HIS MAJESTY

KING GEORGE V.

ADMIRAL OF THE FLEET

BY

His most humble and obedient servant

Willoughby Verner

CONTENTS.

PART I.

The Battle Cruisers at the Action of the Falkland Islands.

		PAGE
Chapter I.—Introduction		1
„ II.—Commander Verner's Narrative of the Action		5
„ III.—Report of Action from German Point of View		14
„ IV.—Notes on the Control of Fire		20
„ V.—After the Action		24

PART II.

	PAGE
Memoir of Rudolf Henry Cole Verner. By Harold Hodge	31
Epilogue. By Ida Verner	65
Appendix I.—Last Hours	67
„ II.—Letters	71
„ III.—Official "Mentions"	80
„ IV.—The Subsequent War-History of the *Inflexible*	81
„ V.—A German Account of the Action of the Falklands	82

LIST OF ILLUSTRATIONS.

		PAGE
1.	Portrait of Commander Rudolf Henry Cole Verner	*Frontispiece*
2.	Enemy approaching Port William, Falkland Isles. View from Fore Top, *Inflexible*	6
3.	Opening Phase of the Action. Battle Cruisers firing on Enemy retiring. Range 15,000—16,000 yards	8
4.	*Inflexible*, after disabling *Scharnhorst*, engages *Gneisenau*	10
5.	Last Rounds falling about *Scharnhorst*, two minutes after silencing her	12
6.	Impressions of Shell appearance when firing at *Scharnhorst* at 14,000 yards	20

(Nos. 2 to 6 are from water-colour sketches by Commander Verner.)

7.	Rough Plan of the Action off the Falkland Isles, by Commander Verner	30
8. 9.	Photographs taken on the Royal Yacht *Victoria and Albert* by H.M. Queen Alexandra (reproduced by permission)	34
10. 11.	A Drive after Wild Geese in Southern Spain	36
12.	H.M.S. *Inflexible* in Action at the Dardanelles, 25 February 1915	54
13.	H.M.S. *Inflexible* in the Attack on the Narrows, Dardanelles, 18 March 1915	60
14.	Lowering the Wounded from the Fore-Control Top of *Inflexible*	62
15.	Fore-Control Top of *Inflexible* after the Action	62
16.	Memorial Window to Commander Verner in the English Church at Algeciras, Spain	65

PART I.

THE BATTLE CRUISERS AT THE ACTION OF THE FALKLAND ISLANDS.

CHAPTER I.

INTRODUCTION.

ONE of the most dramatic incidents in the Great War was the dash of the two Battle Cruisers, the *Invincible* and the *Inflexible*, from the North Sea to Cape Horn, some 7,000 miles, to seek out and destroy the German squadron under Vice-Admiral Graf von Spee which had shortly before sunk the *Good Hope* and *Monmouth* with the gallant Cradock and all hands off Coronel on the west coast of South America.

It is unnecessary to dwell here on the extraordinary importance of the timely arrival of these fine ships under Vice-Admiral Sir Doveton Sturdee, for without their aid the British Squadron of Light Cruisers in the South Atlantic would have been scattered and destroyed by the powerful armoured cruisers *Scharnhorst* and *Gneisenau*, owing to the vastly superior armament and high speed of these ships. Further, but for the victory of the Falkland Islands von Spee would have inflicted incalculable damage alike on our trade in the Atlantic and our credit among the neutral nations, who at this time were waiting carefully to see whether Great Britain retained her supremacy at sea under modern conditions of warfare.

That the victory came at an opportune moment is now admitted by all the world, for at the time there was some anxiety as to the security of our naval position. We must ever bear in mind that it was over 100 years since Trafalgar—the last time that a British fleet fought a general action with an enemy. The public too, necessarily ignorant of naval science were, as always, impatient at what seemed to be excessive delay in asserting our Navy's predominance in every sea and at all times.

The Battle Cruisers at the Falklands

The bitterness of the defeat of Sir Christopher Cradock's small squadron at the hands of Graf von Spee on 1 November and the knowledge that, owing to the mistakes of some of our Naval advisers, the *Good Hope* and *Monmouth* had been hopelessly outclassed and overwhelmed by the *Scharnhorst* and *Gneisenau*, had sunk deep into the heart of the nation. Great therefore was the rejoicing when it was announced that on 8 December, 1914, Sturdee had sent to the bottom the German squadron and Cradock was avenged. For a time the public gave up repeating the silly cry "What is our Navy doing?"

It is interesting to recall that although the (displacement) tonnage of Nelson's ships at Trafalgar was not more than approximately 90,000, at the Action of the Falkland Islands, which was one between two squadrons only, that of the British ships engaged was over 74,000 tons. Of course no parallel is drawn between the relative importance of the two fights, but the figures alone show the extraordinary development of sea-warfare in the 100 years' interval separating them.

On the outbreak of the war my son had the good fortune to be Gunnery Lieutenant as well as 1st Lieutenant of the *Inflexible* and was thus in the most favourable position to see and to describe any fighting that took place.

I was at Gibraltar in January, 1915, when the *Invincible* and *Inflexible* came there to repair damages received at the Falklands Action a month earlier. During the few days my son was at the Rock he naturally told me much about his recent experiences and more especially about the German Officers whom the *Inflexible* had rescued after the sinking of the *Gneisenau* and who had been, for some time, prisoners on board of his ship. He told me how he had from time to time made notes of their conversations with him and had discussed with them the various phases of the action and had shown them the notes he had made, which they had read carefully and had agreed *were absolutely correct*. The originals of these notes came into my possession when his papers were sent to me some months later, after his death in action in the attempt to force the Dardanelles on 18 March, 1915, and formed the basis upon which he had written certain reports of a confidential nature. I naturally kept these reports private during the war but the complete destruction of the German Fleet has rendered this no longer necessary. No one now can suffer from their publication. However, I submitted them to the Admiralty and received full permission to publish them. It is of interest that upon their receipt by the Admiralty early in 1915 these reports, and much else of a technical nature which my son had embodied, was printed in a "secret" paper and issued confidentially to the Fleet.

Introduction

The reports here given undoubtedly contain much information which *at the time* they were written was but little known to the Service in general. An Admiral whom I met at the United Service Club upon my return to England in 1915 said to me : " Your son's reports have told us more about the actual fighting of a warship under modern conditions than any other account we have received." It must always be remembered that in December 1914, when these reports were written and the sketches drawn, the appearance of the various explosives and projectiles when they struck a ship and the effects of fire of heavy guns at the extreme ranges then employed in action for the first time, were matters upon which no precise information was available. Of course the experiences of our Navy in the subsequent sea-fighting from the Dogger Bank onwards have since vastly extended our knowledge of these subjects.

With regard to the coloured sketches reproduced in this book the first one, showing the German Squadron approaching Port Stanley, was on two pages of a sketch-book, each measuring $3\frac{1}{2}$ inches by 5 inches, and was obviously drawn on the spot and coloured later. On the back of this sketch was a rough plan of Port William (also clearly drawn on the spot) which appears in this book at page 6. The remainder of the sketches were done very shortly after the action whilst my son's "impressions" of what he had witnessed were still vivid.

Before giving the description of the action it may be well to summarize briefly the share of the *Inflexible* in the war before she took part in the dash from her patrol work in the North Atlantic (latitude 63° 40' N.) to Cape Horn (51° 10' S.).

The *Inflexible* had been on the Mediterranean Station since 1913. Her Captain was Arthur L. Loxley and she flew the flag of Admiral Sir A. Berkeley Milne, Bart., G.C.V.O., K.C.B.

On war being declared, our Cruisers were ordered to cover the transport of the Algerian Army Corps to France, and to watch the entrance to the Adriatic, avoiding any action in Italian territorial waters. It was during this time that the escape of the *Goeben* and *Breslau* took place, an account of which will be found later in this book, taken from the daily entries in my son's journal.

The Fleet in the Mediterranean was now re-distributed and the three big Cruisers of the "Invincible" class were sent home to join the Battle Cruiser Squadron in the North Sea. The *Inflexible* arrived at Plymouth on 24 August. Here she coaled and docked and sailed on the 28th. During the interval Sir A. Berkeley Milne, who had been Commander-in-Chief in the Mediterranean since 1912, struck his flag at the end of his period in command. On 29 August Captain A. L. Loxley left and was succeeded by the Chief of the Staff, Captain Richard F. Phillimore. Two days later the *Inflexible* was at Scapa.

Throughout the months of September and October the *Inflexible* and *Invincible* took part in the various operations of the Grand Fleet, sweeping the North Sea southward to Heligoland, and were almost incessantly on patrol work extending as far north as the latitude of Iceland.

On 5 November after the news of the destruction of Admiral Sir C. Cradock's Squadron off Coronel reached England the *Inflexible* and *Invincible* were ordered to proceed to Plymouth to prepare for foreign service and sailed the same evening. They arrived at Plymouth on 8 November (having come round to the west of Ireland) and, after taking in stores, provisions and ammunition for themselves, and the other ships they expected to meet, sailed at 7 p.m. on 11 November.

This brings the account of the *Inflexible*'s movements up to the time when my son's story of the action of the Falklands begins.

I should like to call the especial attention of readers to Appendix V at the end of this book, which contains an account of the Action of the Falklands by the Commander of the German cruiser *Gneisenau*, which was published in Germany after the War. A comparison of the two accounts is instructive.

WILLOUGHBY VERNER.

CHAPTER II.

COMMANDER VERNER'S NARRATIVE OF THE ACTION.

THE squadron consisting of *Invincible*, *Inflexible*, *Carnarvon*, *Cornwall*, *Kent*, *Bristol* and *Glasgow* arrived at Port William early on Monday forenoon 7 December, 1914. The *Invincible* and ourselves were at Cromarty on 3 November when news of the action off Valparaiso reached England; that evening we received orders for foreign service and the guess we made as to our probable destination was a good one.

Leaving Plymouth on the 11th, we reached St. Vincent on the 17th and Abrolhos on the 26th, coaling at both places; at the latter finding the remainder of the squadron who were very glad to see us. No definite news of the enemy's movements reached us but it seemed probable that they would sooner or later come east into the South Atlantic, and so we pushed on to the Falkland Islands in the hopes of arriving before they did.

Arriving there, we found the *Canopus* which was doing duty as guardship and generally looking after the defence of the harbour. *Bristol* and *Glasgow* went up harbour to coal and one collier came alongside *Carnarvon*; the *Macedonia*, armed merchantman, remained outside on patrol duty whilst the rest of us prepared for an all-night coaling. We had intended to take our coal from the *Bristol's* collier, but at about 4 p.m. this coal was found to be on fire and the subsequent delay prevented us getting our collier alongside till 6 a.m. Tuesday, the 8th.

At 8 o'clock to breakfast and just as we were turning to again, at 8.30, we received reports of strange men-of-war in sight to the south. Orders for full-speed were issued, and *Kent* and *Glasgow*, which had steam up, were sent outside to keep an eye on things. We carried on coaling but by 9 o'clock two enemy cruisers could be seen from aloft approaching rapidly, so cast off collier, manned the turrets with reduced crews and commenced to shorten-in cable. Whilst doing this, the *Canopus* fired two rounds of 12-inch at the advancing cruisers and "action" was sounded on board of us. I left the forecastle and went up to the fore-top, where I received reports of "ready to open fire" and then cast about for some means of doing so. The enemy were now clearly visible some 18,000 yards away, one large and one small cruiser, whilst on the southern horizon three patches of smoke indicated the position of the remainder of the squadron.

The trouble was that between us and the enemy was interposed a peninsula with irregular outline, and whilst I from aloft had a clear field of view, the guns could see nothing but rocks and sand. Having no director-firing arrangements, I ordered the guns to lay for the dark line at the water's edge (the high-water

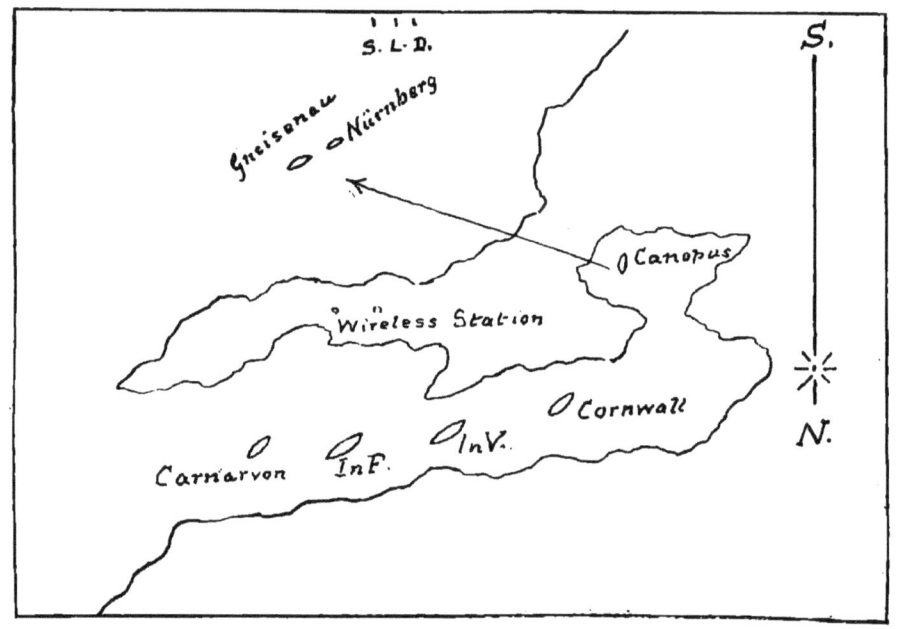

ROUGH PLAN OF PORT WILLIAM, FALKLAND ISLANDS.

Drawn in pencil in pocket-book on back of sketch of "Enemy approaching Port William. View from Fore Top."
InF. = Inflexible, InV. = Invincible, S. = Scharnhorst, L. = Leipzig, D = Dresden.

mark), and passed the "bearing of enemy" in the usual way, but to my very great relief the enemy, after having received two more rounds from *Canopus*, turned east and steamed in the direction of the harbour entrance. After continuing on this course for some fifteen minutes they turned away south-east to join their consorts, and I am very sure that I was not the only one who was glad to see them do so.

My first thoughts on hearing of the enemy's approach were of bewilderment at our enormous good fortune in having arrived in time, and at the enemy having the courtesy to come to us and so save us the long hunt we were

ENEMY APPROACHING PORT WILLIAM, FALKLAND ISLES.

Canopus firing from Port Stanley. View from Fore Top, *Inflexible*, 8.12.14.

The Chase

prepared for. Second impressions were not so cheerful; here we were in harbour, colliers alongside, steam available at about an hour's notice, most of us short of coal and an apparently very enterprising enemy closing us fast.

Indirect fire at moving objects is not an artillerist's ideal, and in any case a squadron getting under way and going out of harbour under fire is not an ardently wished for situation. I had a distinct fellow-feeling with the young man of this neighbourhood of whom the bard has written,* and judging by the cheeriness of everyone else, he must have been in other people's minds as well as my own. However, with the enemy turning away as they did the only thought remaining was as to the number that we could catch, and there was much discussion between ourselves as to their possible speed, the amount of daylight available, etc.

We left harbour at 10.15 a.m., *Invincible*, *Kent*, *Cornwall* and *Glasgow* in company, and could see the enemy some fifteen miles to the south-east steaming in that direction. Chased for a short time and then eased to enable the "County" cruisers to keep up, but at 11 a.m. increased to twenty-two knots with the result that we began to overhaul the enemy and at 11.30 piped to dinner.

At 12.30 p.m. increased speed to twenty-four to twenty-five knots and rapidly came up with the enemy, who were apparently steaming twenty to twenty-one knots. Went up to the bridge and discussed matters with the Captain and decided for a start, to fire at whichever should prove to be the nearest cruiser. The enemy were in line-abreast formation, the *Gneisenau* and *Nürnberg* being on the left of the line (they were the two cruisers which had approached the Island) and then came *Scharnhorst* (flagship), *Dresden* and *Leipzig*. The last-named was rather astern of the remainder and since we were on the starboard side of the *Invincible* and the enemy were a little on our starboard bow, the *Leipzig* became our first target.

1st Phase of Action (12.57 p.m.).

Invincible hoisted the signal to open fire at about 12.55 and at 12.57 we fired the first round of the action at the *Leipzig*. This fell short and I tried again with 16,000 yards on the sights and, as this shot also failed to reach, checked fire and reported enemy out of range. *Invincible* also fired a few rounds at

---

* " There was a young man of Cape Horn,
  Who wished that he'd never been born."

Scharnhorst with like result. The *Kent*, which was on our disengaged side, gave us some unauthorized cheers as we opened fire and it certainly must have been a very pretty picture. A blue cloudless sky above with blue calm sea below, the atmosphere extraordinarily clear (with even low-power glasses it was possible to make out small details of a ship ten miles away), the two Battle Cruisers forcing their way through the quiet sea, white streaks at stems and the water boiling in their wakes, often higher than the after-decks, masses of black oily smoke from the funnels, against which the many ensigns (we were flying five) showed up in striking contrast. Ever and anon, the roar from the forward turret guns and heavy masses of dark chocolate-coloured cordite smoke tumbling over the bows: a long wait and tall white "stalagmites" growing out of the sea behind the distant enemy. After a short while we opened fire again, and this time found the range, though direction was rather troublesome due to the narrow target presented by the end-on enemy, but both *Invincible* and ourselves got very close to the mark; the *Invincible* dropping a shell under the stern of one cruiser, whilst we put one over and so close to *Leipzig* that she was lost from sight as she was steaming through the falling water raised by it.

It was now clearly merely a matter of time, and short at that, before both ships would be hitting with regularity, and this must have occurred to the German Admiral, who ordered "Light cruisers spread and make for American ports, armoured cruisers fight to the end." In response to this signal the two big cruisers turned to port showing their broadsides, whilst the light cruisers continued on their original courses, *Kent*, *Cornwall*, and *Glasgow* in chase. The *Bristol* which had been the last to leave harbour was employed chasing two German colliers which she subsequently sank, and thereby had no chance of taking a hand in the more interesting work. As soon as the armoured cruisers turned, we did likewise and opened fire on them at about 14,500 yards, *Invincible* engaging *Gneisenau*, then leading, and ourselves the *Scharnhorst*.

Whilst waiting for the fall of our ranging salvo, "twinkles" of light and brown "smears" appeared on the forecastle and quarter-deck of enemy, which caused one of my party to ejaculate in evidently intense surprise "They're *firing* at us!" I had leisure to ask him what he thought we had come to Cape Horn for? when our shots fell short, as I think did those from the enemy. Their

INFLEXIBLE INVINCIBLE

OPENING PHASE OF THE ACTION.

Battle Cruisers firing on Enemy retiring. Range 15,000-16,000 yards. Enemy, 1½ points on starboard bow. Wind, Astern.

fire-control struck me as efficient, good salvos, spreading some 200 yards and fired frequently. One could hear their shell before it reached us and after a little practice could tell with certainty if it was one likely to interest us or not. Our own fire was indifferent, or so it struck me at the time; the range was considerable, 14,000-12,000-16,000 yards; a fair number of small alterations of course, considerable amount of smoke from our next-ahead, which, though not sufficient to trouble the gun-layers, made spotting at such ranges difficult. Short shots could not be counted; "hits" and "overs" were hard to see. After some ten minutes shooting the *Scharnhorst* drew ahead and took the lead, necessitating a change of target to *Gneisenau* which had thus become our "opposite number."

Whilst firing at *Scharnhorst* I had only felt confident of two hits; long low walls of water rising to the level of her upper deck, and thought by myself to be water-line or under-water hits. Those on board *Gneisenau* said that when the flagship passed them they saw a large hole in her starboard (or disengaged) side.

To change targets as we did was of course the obvious thing for *Invincible* and ourselves to do, but *Scharnhorst* did not appreciate the need for such action and consequently for a short time we were honoured with the attentions of both ships. I only saw one hit made on *Gneisenau*, but they told us that they received three hits during this portion of the action and that these occurred after changing places with *Scharnhorst* and left them with some fifty wounded men, a poor result from some fifteen minutes' shooting.

2nd Phase of Action (2.5 p.m.).

At about 2 o'clock, the range being then over 15,000 yards and our smoke badly interfering with the gun-laying and control, we drew out of action and I must confess that I did not feel wildly delighted over my share of the performance. This feeling was possibly due to the fact that I was wet through from shell spray and was feeling very cold, and it was most certainly intensified by the enemy continuing to fire at us through our smoke. Several of their shot fell between *Invincible* and ourselves and left yellow-green patches on the surface of the sea, and I well remember watching the stem of the ship driving towards these and wondering whether it were wise or not to pass over such a spot, on the widely known but I believe erroneous principle that no two shots will strike the same place. As a matter of fact only a dozen or so shell fell about us as we followed *Invincible* round, and when I next caught sight of the enemy they were on our starboard quarter steering in the opposite direction to ourselves and some 19,000 yards away. Now followed a wait of some forty minutes or so whilst we made one or two turns to starboard in order to re-engage clear of our smoke. The enemy looked untouched, and, as far as I could see, *Invincible* and ourselves were also undamaged save that the flagship had a hole in her side before "Q" turret and apparently on the stokers' mess-deck. Reports from "quarters" gave the ammunition expended as 150 rounds, and since I was only sure of three hits I hardly felt in a position to remind anyone that we still held the Battle Practice Cup. However, everything else had gone admirably and the much maligned communications had proved completely adequate, possibly because for once in his sinful life everyone concerned was doing his best to hear.

3rd Phase of Action (2.51 p.m.).

See Plan, p. 30.

At three o'clock we again came into action under almost identical conditions as before, save that we now commenced on *Gneisenau*. Spotting was again troublesome since small corrections had no apparent effect and large ones lost us the target. At one period having found and then lost the target, I gave an order of "down 200" and was delighted to see a good straddle and for some time (one minute? five minutes?) watched with much satisfaction a regular deluge of water falling round and about the enemy, when suddenly into the right-hand field of my glasses there crept the stem of another ship and I realized that I had been an admiring spectator of *Invincible's* shooting, during which time our own shots on the *Gneisenau* had remained unspotted. As a matter of fact this discovery was really a relief, since I had been perturbed for the past few minutes because, despite the fact that our shooting appeared good, it seemed to have no effect on the enemy's rate of fire. Two orders of "down 200" speedily took effect and the atmosphere became clearer. By this time (3.20) we were going strong but had to check for two alterations of course of twelve and six points, which being executed together put us in the position of leader, and for the first time I experienced the luxury of complete immunity from every form of interference. Very soon after steadying on this course, the *Scharnhorst*, which had to all appearances received a good hammering from *Invincible*, turned about sixteen points to

INVINCIBLE INFLEXIBLE

INFLEXIBLE, AFTER DISABLING SCHARNHORST ENGAGES GNEISENAU.

Invincible is closing and firing on the sinking Scharnhorst.

starboard and, having got clear of *Gneisenau's* smoke, opened a rapid and well-directed fire on us. This certainly surprised me, since I had looked on her as a beaten ship and despite the alteration of relative positions had intended to continue firing at *Gneisenau*, which we were at that time hitting fairly often. However, *Scharnhorst's* fire had to be replied to and so shifted target and engaged her. We found the range quickly, there was a very small change of range, and so went to "slow independent" (a round per gun per minute).

I was now in a position to enjoy the control-officer's paradise : a good target, no alterations of course and no "next-aheads" or own smoke to worry one. As a matter of fact my perfect enjoyment was marred, because although we were most obviously "all over her" I could not stop her firing, and through the spray of our short shots one could see the "twinkles" of her gun discharges as she continued to fire the most perfect salvos; "rapid independent" ("P" turret had three shell in the air at one time), though apparently accurate, seemed to have no effect and I remember asking my rate-operator "What the devil can we do?" (his answer, though brief, was neither to the point nor repeatable), when *Scharnhorst* suddenly shut up, as when a light is blown out. We continued to fire on her for a minute or two longer and then she turned towards us and we could see that she was listing heavily to starboard, funnels all awry, and on fire forward and amidships. As she was obviously sinking, we checked fire and waited for our old friend the *Gneisenau* (4.5 p.m.).

I had not had leisure to observe how *Invincible* had fared whilst we were arranging matters with the *Scharnhorst*, but I was distinctly annoyed when *Gneisenau* shifted target and fired at us. This struck me as grossly unfair since I was trying to help *Invincible* by firing at her antagonist and had not expected to draw the latter's fire in addition. As a matter of fact *Invincible* had turned to port to give the finishing touches to *Scharnhorst*, and, as *Gneisenau* thought she was going to pick up survivors, she fired at us. All went well for a while, since history was repeating itself, our shell falling all about her and her firing, though rapid and well-laid, suffered from bad spotting, and I had at last grasped the fact that at long ranges (12,000-14,000 yards) it takes *time* to beat a ship and that I had been too impatient for immediate results.

By now (4.10), our old enemy, smoke, was drawing near to the line of bearing, and since a turn to port would have closed the range to less than it had ever been

(10,000-11,000 yards) and made our own smoke more foul, and would moreover foul *Invincible*, which was coming up on our port quarter, we altered course to starboard under the impression that she would follow us round and so across the *Gneisenau's* wake. The flagship however held her course and ordered us to take station astern of her, and so at 4.35 we were back in our old position and worse off than ever. I turned the control over to main-top and "A" turret and back again, but all to no purpose. The *Gneisenau* was now firing at *Invincible* (she could not have seen us) and our gun-layers were firing at the flashes of the enemy's guns seen through *Invincible's* smoke. I did not like to stop them because of a vague feeling that it was probably cheering to the flagship for them to hear us supporting them. Frantic conversation between top and conning tower led to the Captain endeavouring to place the ship on the starboard or weather-bow of *Invincible*, but since she was still steaming fast it soon became evident that this would keep us out of action for a long time and would probably result in our masking *Invincible* with our smoke; so the attempt was abandoned and, turning fourteen points to port, we left the flagship, and at 4.50 ran through her smoke into sunlight.

4th Phase of Action (4.55 p.m.).

Gneisenau looked much the same as ever and was firing with much vigour at *Invincible*, which was apparently sitting tight on her ammunition and firing slowly. Opened fire from our starboard, guns and fired for some ten minutes, range 11,000-13,000 yards, and then, turning twelve points to starboard, had a very satisfactory twenty-five minutes' shoot until she ceased firing, we then being 10,000 yards from her.

Altered course towards the *Gneisenau* under the impression that she had struck, but a few minutes later (5.35) she reopened fire on *Invincible*, so turned away and fired for seven minutes (range 8,000-9,000 yards). Once again the enemy was silenced, but this time we kept off until we were certain as to her intentions and, sure enough, at 5.45 she again opened fire, to which we replied. This was the last round fired at us; as they explained to me afterwards it was "the only undamaged gun in the ship that would bear." Incidentally, it passed over the after-deck and evoked much interest amongst the members of the after-turret's crew who had come up on the roof of the turret "to see what was happening."

LAST ROUNDS FALLING ABOUT *SCHARNHORST*

two minutes after silencing her and just before she turned towards us, on fire, fore and aft, and obviously sinking.

Sinking of the Gneisenau

We fired about ten rounds and then ceased firing and closed *Gneisenau*, which was then listing heavily and sinking. She went over slowly and gave ample time for uninjured men to get on deck (survivors estimate that their were some 300 collected on the forecastle and quarter-deck) before the ship turned over on her beam-ends. In this position she remained for about ten seconds and then quite quietly disappeared from view, the bow remaining above water for a few seconds after the rest of the hull had disappeared. There was no explosion, but steam and smoke continued to rise from the surface and hung in a thin cloud over the spot where she sank.

Within a few minutes we were up to the survivors, some 200 men, supporting themselves with hammocks, belts, spars, etc. *Carnarvon* and *Invincible* joined us speedily and the three ships together saved some 200 officers and men. Later in the day we heard that *Cornwall* and *Glasgow* had sunk the *Leipzig* and that *Kent* had destroyed *Nürnberg*.

A three days' search for *Dresden* and then to Port William to coal. Left this on the 13th and with *Glasgow* and *Bristol* carried out a search of Magellan Straits and the bays and channels round the Horn, and on the 18th when not far south of Valparaiso received orders to return to home waters. We had intended to search Mas-á-fuera (an island near Juan Fernandez) and thence to Valparaiso, but on the 17th we intercepted a signal from *Australia* ordering *Newcastle* to Mas-á-fuera and so decided to remain to the south of it.

For the superstitious it will be interesting to know that on 5 November, 1912, *Inflexible* was commissioned to relieve *Good Hope* as flagship on the Mediterranean station, and that on 5 November, 1914, we received orders which resulted in the action off the Falkland Islands and, further, that the *Scharnhorst* sank the *Good Hope* off Valparaiso, and *Scharnhorst's* last twenty minutes as a man-of-war was spent under the fire of *Inflexible's* guns. We returned to Falkland Isles on the 23rd, coaled and left on the 24th. Arrived at our intermediate coaling rendezvous on the 31st, and left the same afternoon. This was a good day's work, since from midnight to midnight we steamed 200 miles and took in 1,500 tons of coal.

CHAPTER III.

REPORT OF ACTION FROM THE POINT OF VIEW OF *GNEISENAU*
(As described by German officers to Commander Verner).

[*Note.*—The marginal references to "times" have been taken from Commander Verner's notes; they are *not* in the original MS.—Ed.]

2nd Phase of Action.

[About 1.30 p.m.] Leading ship and firing at *Invincible*, *Scharnhorst* astern and firing at *Inflexible*.

[1.40 p.m.] Hit *Invincible* at least once and then *Scharnhorst* passed us and so we engaged *Inflexible*.

This ship struck us three times on upper deck between masts.

[2 p.m.] Enemy drew out of range covered by their own smoke.

See Plan, p. 30.

3rd Phase of Action.

[2.50 p.m.] *Scharnhorst* leading and we engaging *Inflexible*; *Inflexible* firing bad and only one or two hits. *Scharnhorst* received several hits from *Invincible* and altered course sixteen points to starboard; when she passed us we noticed that one funnel was damaged and there was a small fire on board.

[3.30 p.m.] Followed *Scharnhorst* round but turned beyond her so as to avoid the portion of sea which she had passed through.

When we had turned round we opened fire on *Invincible* who was firing at us.

[3.45 p.m.] Ahead of us *Scharnhorst* was receiving a very heavy fire from *Inflexible*, and *Scharnhorst* soon after this turned towards the enemy in a sinking condition, on fire and much damaged.

[4 p.m.] Passed *Scharnhorst* and opened fire on *Inflexible*, who replied giving us several hits.

[4.5 p.m.] Observed *Scharnhorst* sinking astern of us.

4th Phase of Action.

Both of enemy now firing at us but for about half an hour we received few hits.

[4.10 p.m.] *Inflexible* then turned sixteen points and opened fire on us causing very much damage.

By this time we had no steam, light, etc., one turret could not train and three 8·2-inch guns in casemates were out of action.

While *Inflexible* was firing at us from astern we could only fire at *Invincible* and [4.45 p.m.– 5.15 p.m.] could not see her because of her high-explosive shells which fell short.

After a short time we opened fire again on *Invincible* with two 5·9-inch and one 8·2-inch guns (?, R. V.).

Inflexible also fired on us and our remaining guns were put out of action.

Inflexible ceased fire and came towards us. [5.30 p.m.]

Our Captain sent to find if there was any gun that could fire and we found we could [5.45 p.m.] fire one round (the only one left) from the fore-turret at *Inflexible*. This we did and *Inflexible* turned away and fired fourteen or fifteen shots at us, several hitting.

She then ceased fire and closed us just as we sank. [6 p.m.]

NOTES.

Most damage done by shell striking upper deck and pieces going down.

In this way all the 8·2-inch casemates were first disabled and, after this, the 5·9-inch.

The shock caused by shell striking the ship was very great.

All shell seemed to burst, except a few fired at the end.*

Spotting *very* difficult due to enemy's funnel smoke and *cordite* smoke. This was very noticeable when *Inflexible* was firing quickly. Could only see the stem of the ship and the fore-topmast.

NOTE ON THE SURPRISE OF GERMANS AT PRESENCE OF *INVINCIBLE* AND *INFLEXIBLE* AT THE FALKLANDS.

The presence of the Battle Cruisers was an undreamt of possibility.

The *Gneisenau* and *Nürnberg* formed the advance squadron and the Captain of the former would not believe his 1st Lieutenant's report that he could see " two modern cruisers with tripod masts " and it was not till *Canopus* had fired twice that the Captain was convinced. They imagined that *Canopus* was ashore in Magellan Straits and that the *Defence* was the only big ship they were likely to meet. One of their officers, after being brought on board of us asked " Who is this ship ? " And on being told, said " *Inflexible !* you should be in the Mediterranean " !

* Among Commander Verner's notes on gunnery matters is one in which he mentions that in the last Phase of the Action " a few practice projectiles " were fired from one of the turrets; these in his opinion were probably those referred to here.—Ed.

NOTE ON LOSS OF *GOOD HOPE* AND *MONMOUTH* (Action of Coronel).

Scharnhorst engaged *Good Hope* and we the *Monmouth*.

Opened fire at 6.30 p.m., and at 7.15 p.m. *Monmouth* ceased to reply.

Left her and went to assistance of *Scharnhorst*. *Good Hope* had disappeared and we did not know of her loss till reading the report of English Admiralty.

Nürnberg fought *Monmouth* in the dark and sank her with 25—30 shots and might have saved some men but sighted what she thought was *Good Hope* whom she chased and lost.

Scharnhorst received one shell through the bows which did not explode.

Gneisenau received four hits; funnel, turret, and had two men wounded.

Opened fire at 9,000 to 10,000 metres.

NOTES FROM CONVERSATIONS WITH GERMAN OFFICERS.

THEIR methods of control are very similar to our own, save that they place great trust in their range-finders. The 1st Artillery Officer of *Gneisenau* told me that "his largest range-finder was *only three metres*."

This was in the fore lower top; "A" turret and the two battery control positions had one-and-a-half metre range-finders.

The 1st and 2nd Artillery Officers were in the conning tower ("our new ships have separate artillery towers") and in the "plotting room" was the "Battenberg."

The spotting Officers in the upper tops had telegraphs, telephones and voice-pipes to the conning tower and plotting room.

The 1st Artillery Officer was responsible for rate and controlled the 8·2-inch guns. The 2nd Officer endeavoured to keep the 5·9-inch to the 8·2-inch.

The spotters aloft (one on each mast) were kept informed as to the number of guns fired in each salvo in order that they might spot on "the percentage of shots short" principle. All complained bitterly of the difficulty of spotting on us due to our cordite smoke, and stated that this was particularly troublesome when we were firing fast. Lyddite shell bursting short was also troublesome since it raised a "fog." Common shell bursting above the upper deck formed dense clouds of black smoke which "hung" round the ship. Lyddite shell burst with a tremendous noise. All shell hitting caused the ship to "jump," and an Officer aloft told me that he "expected the mast to fall." Much superficial damage was caused by lyddite shell bursting between decks and blowing out the ship's side. When the *Scharnhorst* passed *Gneisenau* during the Second Phase of the action, those on board *Gneisenau* observed "a large hole" on her disengaged side. No shell struck before their foremast and so my three informants could give me no information as to the relative effects on structure or *personnel* of powder-filled and high-explosive shell. One wounded officer we saved had been stationed in the wireless room (in the centre of the 5·9-inch battery) and he said that he had been injured by a shell blowing down the deck above him. His face and hands were mottled by minute scars, and he had also been injured by a falling portion of the deck.

In the Third Phase of the action, after the *Scharnhorst* had sunk, a shell destroyed the casing of the foremost funnel and the fans drew the gases from the funnel into the foremost boiler room, rendering it uninhabitable. About this time a fragment of shell disabled one of the main engines. Much water found its way below, but they consider that this was due to the water which fell on deck and not to under-water injury.

Their Commander, who was picked up by this ship and who apparently had the same general duties as have our Commanders in action, said that "he received information as to where the ship had been struck almost as soon as it happened." (There were two or three telephone stations to his position). Only once did he use a leak stopper, the other damage and fire being caused by shell penetrating the decks.

A shell from *Invincible* struck the front plate of the *Gneisenau's* after-turret and completely wrecked it. Another from *Inflexible* falling on the upper deck burst in an 8·2-inch casemate on the disengaged side and tumbled gun and ship's side-plating into the sea.

Apparently the 8·2-inch casemate guns were the first to be put out of action and this by shell striking the roof. After the upper deck had been broken down, shell were able to burst on or through the roof of the 5·9-inch battery, disabling the guns there, and this process seems to have been repeated down to the armoured deck.

The crews of the 3·4-inch guns (twenty were mounted) were kept below until required to fill vacancies at the larger guns. They were all required.

When the ship finally stopped firing, the state of affairs on board her is well described in the following account given me by the 1st Artillery Officer. I give it as far as possible in his own words.

"The ship stopped firing and my Captain say to me 'Why don't you fire?' I say 'Captain, I cannot, I cannot speak to the guns.' The Captain then sent Lieutenant ——— (the 2nd Artillery Officer) to look. He report that he cannot go round the ship but that he can *see* all the gun and they are disable or have no men. The fore-turret is all right, but has only one round, there is ammunition below but it cannot come up." Owing to the heavy list of the ship this round could not be fired at *Invincible*, and the turrets were trained round and the last shot fired at us, who had ceased firing and were closing an obviously sinking ship. This shell passed over the after-deck and created a keen competition on the part of some of "X" turret's crew, who were on the roof, to return to their action-stations.

The spotting Officer, who had come down to the conning-tower, after his communications were destroyed, remembered that there were life-belts in the top and so climbed up there as the ship was sinking.

He told me that from this point of view the ship between the masts appeared to have no decks down to the armoured one and that this had many large holes in it through which smoke and flame was issuing.

They said that the ship could have floated another hour but that they opened all valves, discharged their lee torpedoes and exploded charges (always placed in all their ships) in the engine-room bilge.

The crew consisted of 780 active ranks and ratings and 80 reservists, and they estimate that there were some 300 alive and mustered on the forecastle and quarter-deck before the ship sank. After the Second Phase over fifty wounded men were collected in their starboard after-hospital, and early in the Third Phase a shell completely destroyed this compartment.

I gathered that their torpedoes when fitted with *warheads* are of negative buoyancy at the beginning and *end* of a run and cannot float. A number of men escaped from below, as the ship heeled over, by climbing through the holes in her side made by our shells.

It will be noticed in the German account* that I have written "light, etc.," after "no steam." This was corrected by them as they had lights from accumulators but not enough voltage to work instruments.

* See p. 14 *ante* under "4th Phase of Action."

Conversations with German Officers

As a possible matter of interest I told them that we heard their 8·2-inch and 5·9-inch shell before they reached us and Lieutenant —— (spotting Officer) stated that the same was noticed by them when *Monmouth* was firing at long range. In the case of 12-inch, however, the shell arrived first. It is evidently a question of final velocities and that of sound.

In the action off Valparaiso the *Gneisenau* fired 200 8·2-inch shell and *Scharnhorst* 400. The 5·9-inch guns were not used. One hundred rounds of 8·2-inch were afterwards transferred to *Scharnhorst* from *Gneisenau* and at the commencement of the last action there were 1,100 rounds of 8·2-inch and 1,200 rounds of 5·9-inch on board each ship.

CHAPTER IV

NOTES ON THE CONTROL OF FIRE.

[The following notes written a few days after the Action of the Falkland Islands throw interesting side-lights on some of the incidents of a modern sea-fight and at the same time describe the personal feelings of an officer engaged in controlling the fire of a big ship. During the five years that have passed since the Action many of the points to which the writer here calls attention have been attended to, the lesson has been learnt and our appliances have been developed and improved. Hence there is nothing here given which can be considered of a confidential nature.—Ed.]

Rate of Fire.

A slow rate of fire was almost impossible to achieve for two reasons. First, owing to the great range and fairly frequent alterations of course, I had the feeling that I was perpetually ranging and had no grip on the target; and secondly, the fact of shell passing close made one anxious to stop the enemy firing, and so to fire rapidly seemed logical.

Before going into action, I had informed officers that one round per gun per minute, when at "independent," would be ample till they received the order to hustle.

Actually, the pole halliards being cut two feet above the fore control-top, produced an order to "blaze away." This occurred when we were hitting *Scharnhorst* hard, but could not stop her fire.

Spotting.

Hits on funnels, masts and upper-works were easy to see; "lyddite" causing a white cotton-woolly cloud, and "common" a dense black one.

Hits on the water-line could be recognized by means of the long low splash raised.

IMPRESSIONS OF SHELL APPEARANCE WHEN FIRING AT *SCHARNHORST* AT 14,000 YARDS. 8.12.14.

Notes on Control of Fire

German reports indicate that all shells burst on striking the water, but I am convinced that a certain number did not, since the column of water thrown up was sometimes precisely similar to that caused by practice projectiles, whilst others were as shown.

Holding the weather position as we did caused the spray from shots short to fall on board the enemy, and led one to think one was hitting.

Shots which fell 100 to 200 yards over could rarely be seen, due to enemy's funnel and cordite smoke, and a rule soon established itself that "down 200" was a sound correction when nothing could be seen.

Deflection caused considerable difficulty, and on two occasions one gun fired some five or six consecutive rounds nearly a ship's length astern of the target. I traced this to a turret and called for the deflection setting, which proved to be correct.

Since this error was intermittent, and always took effect in the same direction, I am convinced that it was due to the gun-layer mistaking the stem for stern, or foremast for mainmast.

The particular cruisers we were engaging made such an error particularly easy, due to the symmetrical arrangements of their masts and funnels.

For myself, I started badly by getting wet to the skin, as the result of a shell falling on the weather-bow. Inability to keep on the target when found, together with irritation at the interruption due to *Invincible's* smoke, alterations of course, and enemy's short shots, made me first cross, and, then, casual.

I think that I controlled best when the enemy was shooting well, since the importance of the latter became so very obvious.

When we became "leading ship" and after we had separated from *Invincible*, all difficulties vanished and I should have been quite happy had I realized that we were firing at considerably longer ranges than in previous battle practices, and that a ship takes longer to destroy than does a target.

Communications were completely satisfactory.

When the enemy were firing *at* one, the discharge of their guns caused a *twinkling* effect, and this changed to a *flash* when their fire was directed at *Invincible*.

CONCLUSIONS.

Matters of Fact.

(1) That low velocities and high elevation, as found in German guns and mountings, enable an accurate and damaging fire to be opened at a very long range. Their 8·2-inch turret guns put salvos over and across us at the end of Phase II, when we could not reply (16,200 yards on our sights).

(2) That the German semi-A.P., i.e. A.P. shell with H.E. burster is a useful shell and combines the advantages of "common" and "lyddite."

(3) That the small splinters from H.E. shell are easily stopped, and that all control positions and anti-torpedo-craft guns should be protected by thin high-tensile steel plating.

(4) That the space between the turret redoubts and turntable, now covered by the apron, is a source of weakness and that the apron should be protected by horizontal plating. In the battle off Valparaiso the *Gneisenau* had a turret put out of action from a portion of 6-inch shell from *Monmouth* entering here.

(5) Respirators were of great value and enabled control parties to remain at their stations; and turrets, where air-blast failed, were able to carry on without opening the armoured hatch.

(6) Heating of paint on gun-jackets seriously inconvenienced gun-layers and trainers by reason of the fumes given off.

(7) The present fire-gong (Siemens' type) is not loud enough and becomes ineffective after much rapid firing, and salvos are difficult to obtain.

Matters of Opinion.

(1) That a senior Officer, Commander or Lieutenant-Commander, should be detailed to watch the fire-effect, and decide whether the fire should be fast, or slow, or checked. He should also be responsible for the selection of target. At present the Captain cannot give *all* his attention to this matter and does not like to interfere with the control officer. Similarly, the control officer, who may be dissatisfied with the shooting, does not like to check fire without orders, or he may become obstinate and continue firing when he should stop.

Conclusions

An officer, who is responsible neither for the handling of the ship, nor the *accuracy* of fire, will have leisure to deal with this problem.

(2) Our system of counting hits on canvas has led us to ignore the virtual and very vulnerable target.

(3) In ships with director-firing, it would be well worth while to wait for the enemy's salvo, and to fire just before their shell arrive. This would take advantage of the smoke protection afforded by the simultaneous discharge of many large guns.

(4) That a time-of-flight instrument is a great help. (We have an electrical machine which operates a rattler in the control position.)

(5) That all persons in sighting hoods and look-out positions, who are not using glasses, should wear splinter-proof spectacles as designed for motorists.

(6) That a range-finder without a control officer is of less value than the converse, and that *adequate* splinter-proof protection should be built in control tops, even if this means the disestablishment of the range-finders.

(7) That a ship without *topmasts* is almost impossible from a range-taking point of view.

(8) That the dense volumes of smoke caused by the combined use of coal and oil at a speed above the ship's designed one will render the weather position impossible in the case of *fleets*.

(9) That we must make up our minds that no German ship will haul down her colours, and that to go to the assistance of a disabled enemy will not protect us from the attentions of any others in the neighbourhood.

[*End of Commander Verner's Notes.*]

[In view of the fact that Commander Verner met his death directing the fire of the *Inflexible* in her fire-control station in the fore-top within three months of writing these notes, it is of considerable interest to read that his experiences at the Falkland Islands had made him fully aware of the extreme vulnerability of the control stations of our ships and their consequent liability to be put out of action. He calls attention to this both as a "Matter of Fact" (No. 3) and as a "Matter of Opinion" (No. 6).—Ed.]

CHAPTER V.

AFTER THE ACTION.

For some days after the Action, as we have seen, the Squadron was engaged in the fruitless search after the *Dresden*. It was on the morning of the 10th that Admiral Sturdee made the following Signal to the Captain of the *Inflexible*.

From	To
Commander-in-Chief	Captain, *Inflexible*.

Date 10.12.14.   Time 10.7 a.m.

I must apologize for having inadvertently omitted to answer your kind congratulations. I feel that after thanking the enemy for his desire to visit the Falklands and honouring us by meeting us there, the welcome given by everyone was most enthusiastic. I owe everything to Engine-Room departments and to the good Gunnery of the ships and thank the *Inflexible* for their great assistance in our serious encounter.

When the *Inflexible* and *Invincible* were at Gibraltar in January 1915 the Editor saw the officers of both ships and heard from them many stories of the German prisoners they had picked up. These tales had for the most part been told them by the German officers, but there were many others which had reached them through our Warrant and Petty officers who had heard them from the survivors of the *Gneisenau's* crew. Naturally such tales must be received with caution but here and again there were accounts of incidents which, to judge from other facts known to be correct, were credible. Among them was that of the German officer who, when the *Gneisenau's* stokehold began to get flooded, shot or threatened to shoot some of the stokers who abandoned their work and made a dash for the ladders. It is useless to speculate whether this officer, as was so freely asserted, was thrown into the furnace or met his fate some other way, but the unanimous verdict was that "*he* did not come on deck again."

Another widely-known tale was the hatred the men had for their Commander and the openly expressed regret of some that they had not had an opportunity to settle accounts with him whilst they were struggling in the water after the *Gneisenau* had disappeared. It was popularly believed that one of the drowning German officers, when picked up, still grasped his automatic pistol and the story runs that when one of our boats reached him and he raised his arm to be pulled on board, a Bluejacket, seeing the pistol still in his hand, gave him a "clip" over the wrist under the belief that he was still showing fight!

When the Editor was lunching one day on board the *Inflexible* at Gibraltar, there was a good deal of chaff about what the officers derisively called "Verner's pal"—the same Commander of the *Gneisenau*—whom they declared to be a most "impossible" person and an embodiment of the very worst "Prussian" type of officer. Verner vigorously defended his line of conduct and declared that he had thereby obtained from this officer much useful information. Of this there is ample proof. All the same he admitted that the Commander made himself most objectionable during his stay on board in spite of the great consideration with which he was treated. He signalized his departure by taking with him a Lieutenant's best great-coat who had been weak enough to lend it to the Commander!

The mind of German officers of this type can be gathered from the following. Verner asked what could have given rise to the tale, as reported in some of the English papers, that in the Heligoland affair (August, 1914) the German officers had shot with their pistols at their men struggling in the water who had jumped overboard from their sinking ship? The reply he received was "*Of course* they had" for "*had they not deserted their ship?*"

However, not all were like this and Verner became good friends with them and more especially with one, who after Verner had fallen in the Battle of the Narrows, wrote in admiration of him to his father from the Prisoners' of War Camp at Holyport.*

What however impressed Verner more than anything else was the German Naval Officers' emphatic and unanimous statement that when they received the news that Great Britain had allied herself with France, they could hardly believe their senses. In their own words it was to them "absolutely incredible" that Englishmen could ever have become the Allies of so degenerate a race as the French. He added that the genuineness of their belief was unquestionable, for they were profoundly convinced of the immeasurable superiority of the German race over the French and Russian. In his own words, it was simply hopeless to discuss the point with them. No more significant tribute could be paid to the great position occupied by the British race in the German mind and none the less so that it was divulged thus unconsciously and was most certainly unintended.

In justice to the other officers, one should add that they told Verner that the

---

* This letter is given in Appendix II at end of book.

Commander of the *Gneisenau* was disliked by all his brother officers and was absolutely hated by his men. From the preceding notes and much else one heard this is hardly to be wondered at. The Commander since his return to Germany has published an account of the Action of the Falkland Islands which, making due allowance for his not unnatural glorification of everything Prussian and also, at places, for his "flights of fancy" which can easily be detected, is of interest when compared with the account given in this book. A translation from it is given in an appendix.*

Various writers, mostly non-naval, unaware of the information and evidence in existence, have from time to time cast doubts on several of the points elicited by Verner, more especially on the statement that the *Gneisenau* could have floated another hour and was sunk by the Germans themselves and, further, that all the German warships were prepared for sinking in the event of an action going against them. Of this, as of the accuracy of the statement that the "*Nürnberg* might have saved some men" when the *Monmouth* was sunk, so far as documentary evidence is concerned, there is complete proof.

Needless to say, Verner received many letters from his old shipmates of earlier days. These all struck the same note: pleasure that he should have won his promotion and gratification at his having had the opportunity to put his skill at gunnery to such a practical test and with such overwhelming results. The following letter from Captain A. Schomberg Currey, R.N., D.S.O., one of his old shipmates in the *Albemarle* (on which ship, owing to his youthfulness, he was known as "The Kid") is typical.

H.M.S. *Marlborough*,
1st Battle Squadron,
3 Jan. '15.

DEAR KID,—Please accept my heartiest congratulations on your well-deserved and well-earned promotion and also on the magnificent way you put those swine under. You were lucky to get a smack at them and being Gunnery Lieut. you had all the fun of the fair. Give my chin-chin to the Colonel when you write. I know how pleased he will be. So long, old bird, and best of luck in the future.

Yours ever,
A. SCHOMBERG CURREY.

The following letter was in answer to a friend who wrote congratulating Verner on his promotion and asking for more particulars of the fight. It was sent to the Editor by the recipient some months later—after Verner's death.

* Appendix V.

After the Action

(Written from Malta.) H.M.S. *Inflexible*,
31.1.15.

. . I was very certain when I last saw you (in November) that we should get them, but it was very pleasant to be able to do this job so quickly.

The ship was first class and I am a very contented man. It falls to the lot of few to be able to put two years of strenuous work to the proof and obtain such irrefutable evidence as to the value of one's theories.

I was delighted to hear that our friend C—— had had a rub at them.* The North Sea is hardly big enough to *destroy* big ships by gunfire when the range is great.

We picked up 11 officers and 55 men from *Gneisenau* (much against the will of our men) and I must say the whole afternoon's work left *no* impression on my mind (save technically). I was sometimes peevish when I could not reduce the volume and accuracy of their fire (which was both great and good) but this was induced chiefly by considerations of personal safety.

Scharnhorst we left to sink and saved no one from, but *Gneisenau* (the last to go) sank some 15 minutes after we ceased firing and so we were able to get close up to her before she vanished and within 5 minutes we were in the midst of her men and wreckage.

I came down from aloft and saw that our people were hoisting out boats, etc. (as a matter of fact we only had two boats that could float) and so went down to the wreck of the wardroom, and salved some whiskey which I badly needed (I had been wet through and very cold for the past six hours) and then made a tour of the guns to see how they were. Meantime other ships had closed and between us we saved some 200 officers and men.

I must admit that I felt absolutely unconcerned as to whether we saved one or a thousand and I was able to watch ships and men go under with no sort of emotion. And I have always cursed myself for being emotional.

The *Scharnhorst* sank after half an hour's shooting at 13,000 yards ($7\frac{1}{3}$ land miles).

We are now on another jaunt not quite so far afield as the last one.

* * * * *

Yours ever, RUDOLF.

The following account written by one of the turret gun-layers in the *Inflexible*, which appeared in the newspapers in January 1915, gives a good idea of the course of the Action from the point of view of the lower deck.

. . . . . The *Scharnhorst* now opened fire on us and we on her but after a few of our pills she took up position ahead of the *Gneisenau*. I don't know if she found things uncomfortable. . . . . So now we fired at the *Gneisenau* and gave her a hot time, she firing hard at us but her shells were falling short and some over us, passing between the masts but doing no damage.

The German ships turned round and so did we, and this time we had the *Scharnhorst* for our target. We now got her range nicely, and we put it across her just right, so that she was soon in difficulties. We could see her funnels fall, first one and then another until she only had half of one left out of the four. Her firing was getting slack and her topmast and colours were

---

* Alludes to Action of 24 January 1915 near the Dogger Bank when the *Blücher* was sunk.

shot away but they hoisted them again. About now she was on fire in about three places and her side seemed to be split abreast. Where her first and second funnels had been, a cloud of steam went up, telling us we had found her boilers. Her speed slackened and she was listing very badly. At times we could not see her, as the smoke of our shells bursting on and around her hid her from us. She turned towards us, heeled over and sank very quietly at 4.10. No survivors.

Exit Number One, the pride of the Kaiser. She was his best shooting ship and he presented a Gold Cup to her for her marvellous shooting. I reckon she took that with her; we did not stop to enquire. She could shoot; so can we, and our Cup for the best shooting ship of the Mediterranean for two years is still in safe keeping.

During this time the *Invince* had been engaging the *Gneisenau*, so we now turned to assist her and when we looked at the *Gneisenau* through our telescopes we found she was standing the action very well, in fact she looked quite fresh. Well, we now opened fire on her. Not long after we saw one of her 8-inch turrets go clean over the side, then her foremast funnel fell back on the second one. She was dodging about fairly well, we after her. She was now receiving the fire of both ships and feeling pretty bad I should say, as she got out of range and we were hampered by the *Invince's* smoke so we had to turn right round to get away from it. We now engaged her again and soon she began to list to port. Then she ceased fire, so we closed on her. Then she opened fire again. So did we, and we put the last twelve rounds right into her, so that she heeled over and sank very quietly, just as the *Scharnhorst* had done.

Exit Number Two. We now got out what boats we had intact and we saved eight officers and fifty-five men. The officers complimented our Gunnery Officer on his rapid rate of fire, also the rate of hits he put into her, so that speaks well. I am glad to say that since the action the Gunnery Officer has been promoted and we are all very glad, as he deserves it. The only thing is, we don't want to lose him.

Now we must give the *Gneisenau* and *Scharnhorst* a bit of praise, as they both put up a splendid fight, though they had great odds against them. They were good fighters and fought to the last.

All who are acquainted with the general course of the Action or who read the accounts of it here given will agree that in the preceding narrative there is very little to find fault with. It is obviously written in entire good faith and describes the various incidents of the fight as they appeared to the men fighting the guns.

This account appeared in *The Evening News* and after the manner of the daily papers it was headed in extra large type "'Pride of the Kaiser,' The *Inflexible's* Victim."

Apparently this somewhat harmless embellishment caused some comment; at any rate some futile discussion arose as to the relative shares of the two Battle Cruisers in their joint action.

This led to the following letter from Verner to Admiral Henderson written on 4 March 1915. Verner had given his father when at Algeciras in January his account of the Action which appears in this book and, after saying that he had obtained permission

After the Action

from his Captain to publish it, had asked that it might be forwarded to Admiral W. H. Henderson (Editor of the *Naval Review*) for that purpose. This was done and the MS. was duly received and put into type.

Meanwhile the *Inflexible* proceeded to the Dardanelles and a mischievous report was spread that some one in the *Inflexible* had been attempting to minimize the part in the fight taken by the *Invincible*. The outcome of this was that when Verner was at Malta in March, he wrote the following letter to Admiral Henderson who most kindly sent it to the Editor.

It was one of the last letters Verner ever wrote.

"H.M.S. *Inflexible*,
Mediterranean Fleet,
14.3.15.

DEAR ADMIRAL HENDERSON,—Thank you for your letter. Since receiving it there have come to our ears the rumours that *Invincible* is labouring under the delusion that officers of this ship have written about the Falkland Action in a manner calculated to discredit our late Flagship. This is, as far as I know, the veriest nonsense and in any case I am sure her conscience is at least as good as ours and must be proof against such futile wrangles as to "who did worst." Under these circumstances my Captain considers that my little account were best unpublished.

I have not seen it for two months and cannot be certain that there is nothing of a nature which could add fuel to flame. If you would kindly re-read it from that point of view, I am sure I may count on your judgment.

The account was written for (*a*) Service friends who could supplement the information given by means of Official reports, and (*b*) friends and relatives, and if it should appear to be 'above suspicion' its publication *might* do more good than harm. So sorry to thus trouble you.

Yours very truly,
RUDOLF VERNER."

It is satisfactory to record that the two ships became good friends again long before they served together in the Battle of Jutland. The Editor has the authority of Commander Dannreuther, the Gunnery Officer of the *Invincible* at the Falklands and at Jutland, for his statement.

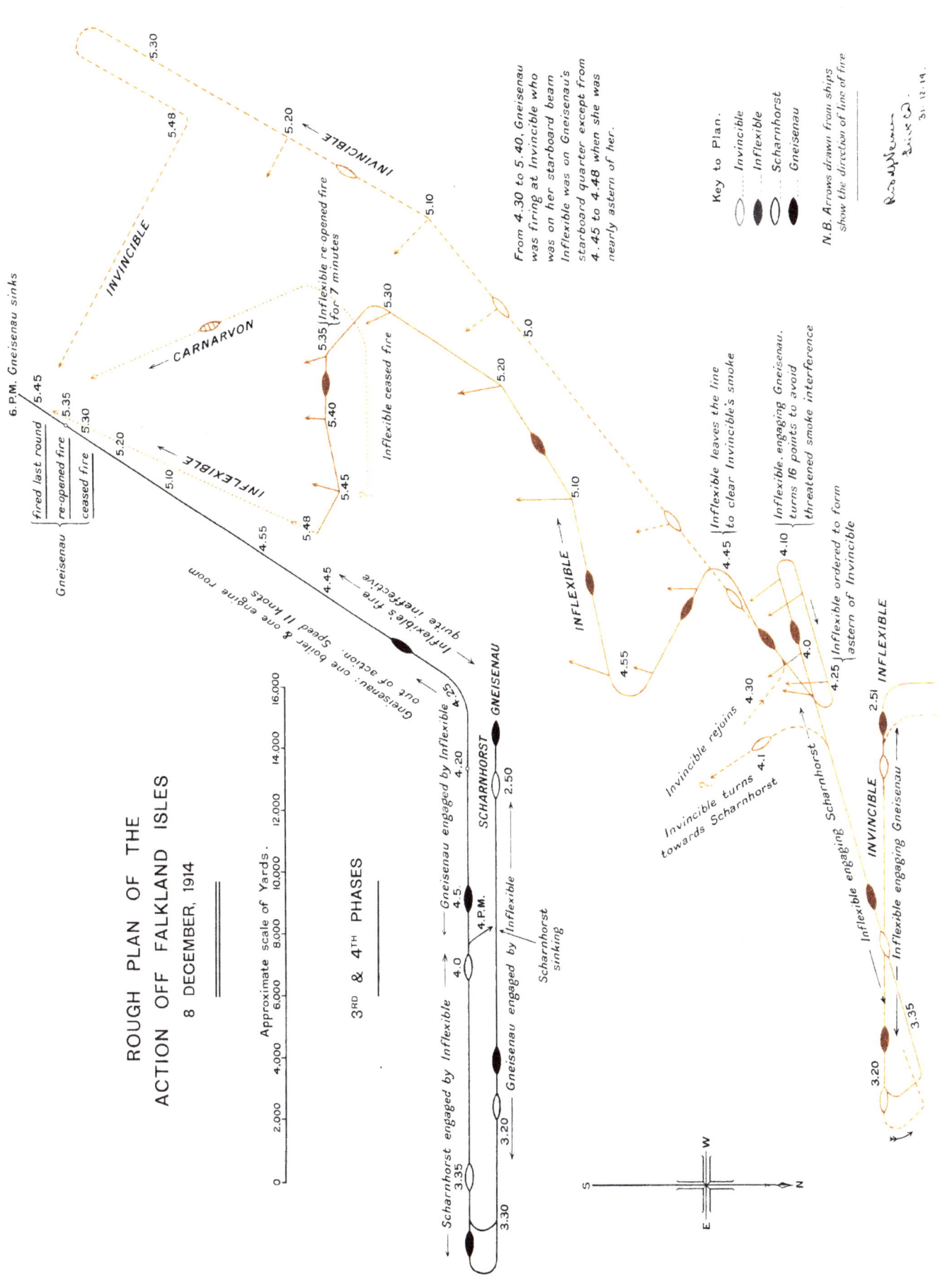

PART II.

Memoir of
RUDOLF HENRY COLE VERNER.

By HAROLD HODGE.

THOSE who knew Rudolf Verner well are not likely to forget him; they need no written memorial of his life; but after all a man's intimates are few; and those who knew Verner less well will like to know more of him; and some of those who never met him will not be sorry of an opportunity to read this very brief story of one of the finest fellows that ever lived. If this seems the emotional language of a close friend, at any rate it is certain that every one who knew Verner well would say the same, and though his life was a short one, he managed (quite in his father's way) to get a great deal into it, and his work was public work.

There is always an attraction about a brilliant young officer, which is wonderfully enhanced when the martial bearing is eased off by an easy manner and frank address. Rudolf Verner, or "Dodo" as his intimates generally called him, was more than frank; he had all the qualities, without and within, that tradition describes as "sailor-like"; and his countenance strikingly agreed with them. There was such transparent honesty and kindliness in his face that probably many, who never got to know him at all, thought they knew him core-through on meeting him for the first time. In society and among sportsmen he was popular; but to say he was "generally popular" would be a mis-description; for he was wholly careless of shocking people (perhaps he rather liked to shock them) and troubled himself about the opinion, good or bad, only of those whom he regarded. He was certainly trying to solemn folk, who thought he lacked seriousness, whereas he was so really serious that it was impossible for him to be solemn. This kind of man can talk flippantly of deep things because he is too much with them to be oppressed by them. If such a man has the right kind of home (as Verner had), he will best be understood there. Thus, although Rudolf Verner, like most sailors and, for that matter, most men of action, was essentially religious, his religion was not on the surface. It could be felt by the sympathetic; one simply knew it was there; but the unsympathetic might think he knew the opposite. Yet to such a man the world without God was inconceivable.

The peculiar point about Verner's personality was that he was a blend of the hard-bitten man of action and the intellectual, of the philistine and the artist. This is not common, for the two temperaments find it difficult to accommodate each other. To most people Verner would no doubt appear just a fine specimen of his class, the well-known (and invaluable) English type; but he really belonged as much to the study as to the field. He was never happier than when pondering some new idea in connexion with his profession. Probably the greatest delight in life to him was to see how some theory of his own worked out in practice. Fortunately this joy came to him more than once in his own sphere of naval gunnery. He was a ceaseless thinker—it may be he thought a little too much—and yet he was also a good talker—from discussion to story telling. His good temper and keen sense of humour helped him in both. On the whole this was a versatile and most lovable man, who gave every power and every gift he had unreservedly to the great Service to which his father and mother had devoted him from his birth, and which he loved passionately. He lived for the Navy just as he died for it.

Commander Verner came from a fighting stock, being the son of Colonel Willoughby Verner of the Rifle Brigade, and the Hon. Elizabeth Mary Emily Parnell, fourth daughter of the third Lord Congleton. Colonel Verner served on Lord Wolseley's Staff in the Sudan Expedition 1884-85, being in the Desert March and at the action of Abu Klea and later in Gordon's steamers on the Nile. He was on the Headquarters Staff in the South African War 1899-1900, and was at the actions of Belmont and Graspan, where he received such severe injuries that he was compelled to retire from the Service with a wound pension. Colonel Verner's father, Colonel William John Verner, served in the 53rd and 21st Regiments and his great-uncle, Colonel Sir William Verner (7th Hussars), served under Moore in the Coruña Campaign and in the Peninsular War and was severely wounded at Waterloo. Mrs. Willoughby Verner's father served in the Royal Navy and as a Midshipman was present in H.M.S. *Glasgow* at Navarino. Her brother, the 4th Baron, was in the Buffs, serving in the Crimea and commanding his Battalion in the Zulu War. His eldest son, Rudolf's cousin, the 5th Baron, in the Grenadier Guards,

Early Years

was killed near Ypres in November 1914; his younger son William, also in the Grenadiers, being killed in 1917.

Rudolf Henry Cole Verner was born on 16 January 1883 at his grandfather's house, 13, Bryanston Square, London. At the age of 9 he went to S. Paul's College, Stony Stratford and thence to J. C. Tregarthen's, the Naval coach, at Stratford-on-Avon; and passed into the *Britannia* in April 1897. In July 1898 he passed out seventh in his batch, taking the second prize in Seamanship, and in the following September was appointed Midshipman in H.M.S. *Majestic*, Battleship, 14,900 tons, Captain Prince Louis of Battenburg, the Flagship of the Channel Fleet, commanded by Admiral Sir Henry Stephenson. For a year he went on the usual Channel Squadron cruises. Being at Gibraltar for nine days in April 1899 he made a gallant attempt to win the Midshipmen's Point-to-Point race, borrowing a pony from the Grenadier Guards. In fact he came in first, but unfortunately passed the winning-post on the wrong side, and was disqualified; most of the field following him to the same fate. The silver cigarette case went to a cautious youth who rode in the wake of the field and had time, seeing what happened, to amend his course and pass between the flags.

Even so early in his career young Verner showed a disposition for gunnery, his log containing unusually good drawings of breech-actions and mountings of various guns; and his aptitude for and keen interest in mechanical construction, which he had shown as a mere child, became marked. His Commanding Officer, Prince Louis, notes in his certificate (June 1899) Verner's "great attention and intelligence."

In September 1899 he was appointed to the *Andromeda* (Protected Cruiser, 11,000 tons—then one of the largest of the class) one of the Mediterranean squadron. In the following year the cruiser visited the Riviera and "Dodo" stayed with his parents at the Empress Eugénie's villa at Cap Martin where he caused much merriment by his naval urbanity. During a subsequent visit to H.M. he made the acquaintance of the Princess Ena (the present Queen of Spain).

It was while Rudolf was in the *Andromeda* that he made his first visit to the Dardanelles—he made his last in 1915. On 5 September 1900 he was lent to H.M.S. *Speedy*, the Admiral's Despatch boat, as acting Sub-Lieutenant in place of an officer away sick. His journal at this time shows inherited power of draughtsmanship in many excellent plates of the warships of all classes, both British and French, which he came across. His knowledge of foreign types of warships grew extensive and was well-known, so that he was frequently called upon to identify distant foreign ships. He remained in the *Speedy* only until 25 October following (1900) when he was transferred to H.M.S. *Renown*, Battleship, Captain the Hon. H. Tyrwhitt, the Flagship of the Mediterranean Squadron, of which Admiral Sir John Fisher was Commander-in-Chief, and on her recommissioning 18 November was reappointed to her and served in her until 14 March 1902. At this time his uncle, Major-General Lord Congleton, was commanding the Infantry Brigade at Malta, so Verner had good opportunity of seeing the island and military life. An amusing story is told in connexion with the visit of Their Majesties (at that time T.R.H. the Duke and Duchess of York) to Malta during their tour of the Empire in the *Ophir*; the Fleet, of course, was illuminated and the Admiral received Their Royal Highnesses on his Flagship, the *Renown*. Having duly presented his officers, he called up and presented "my senior Midshipman, Mr. Verner," when H.R.H. the Duchess was good enough to say to him, "I hear you are the smartest midshipman in the Fleet!" "So they tell me, ma'am" answered Mr. Verner (age 17½) with a grave "inclination," as the Court Guide might say. "Dodo" was always able to be audacious without offending. Every one was much amused and the story went round the world with the *Ophir*. This recalls a remark of Sir Berkeley Milne when Commodore of the Royal Yacht, in which Rudolf was serving a few years later, to his uncle, Lord Congleton. "I don't know what the deuce the boy used to tell the Royalties but whenever I came on deck he was surrounded by a crowd of Empresses, Queens and Princesses, all in convulsions of laughter."

On 15 March 1902 Verner was appointed Acting Sub-Lieutenant and was sent home in H.M.S. *Aurora*, his father being on board as the guest of the captain. Capt. Tyrwhitt said of him in his leaving certificate "a promising young officer."

On 29 April Verner joined the Royal Naval College at Greenwich, was appointed in October to H.M.S. *Excellent* for a course of Gunnery, and in the following year 24 March 1903, was appointed to the Royal Yacht *Victoria and Albert*, Rear-Admiral the Hon. Hedworth Lambton, shortly succeeded by Commodore Sir A. Berkeley Milne, Bart. He was in the Royal Yacht until the following October, barring a brief interval in the summer when he was lent to the *Shark*, Destroyer. On leaving the Royal Yacht when he was twenty years and nine months old, he was promoted to Lieutenant with seniority of 31 August 1903. He had taken four out of five possible "firsts" in his exam. so it was not much that service on the Royal Yacht could do for him in the way of time. It is a

PHOTOGRAPHS TAKEN ON BOARD THE ROYAL YACHT *VICTORIA AND ALBERT* BY H.M. QUEEN ALEXANDRA, 1903.

(FROM LEFT TO RIGHT.—SUB-LIEUT. SETON, SUB-LIEUT. VERNER, COLONEL BROCKLEHURST.)

good comment on the value of examinations as a test of ability that Verner's only "second" was in "Seamanship," the branch of his profession in which he was especially efficient, as all his captains testify. During the years he was at Greenwich and Portsmouth he spent most of his leave at his home at Hartford Bridge near Winchfield and, save when shooting, devoted himself to his favourite occupation of building models of battleships and cruisers which no sooner were completed and launched than they were ruthlessly destroyed by mines and gunfire. From his very earliest days as a small lad this making of models of ships from the most intractable and unlooked for materials had engrossed every hour or his play time. These were shot at by every species of toy gun, gradually developing into more deadly weapons, such as saloon rifles, etc. In his *Britannia* days, when his father was on the Staff, the lake at the Royal Military College, Sandhurst, was the scene of constant explosions ot mines to the no small annoyance of some of the passers by. The old gardener at his home, when he heard of Verner's early promotion to Lieutenant said, "I always knew Mr. Rudolf would get on : he was so mortal fond of hexplosives."

Later whilst serving on the Gunnery Staff at Portsmouth, he organized regular ship actions against shore batteries in "mined" waters on the lake at Minley Manor, the house of his great friends Mr. and Mrs. Laurence Currie. The "batteries" were built on commanding promontories and his "cruisers" were of six and eight feet on the keel, built for the occasion. These were armed with Roman candles whose discharge simulated the fire of the guns, and an arrangement of crackers and other fireworks, all connected up by an elaborate system of time-fuses, represented respectively the bursting of shells striking the ships and the fire of the secondary armament. Mine-fields were laid, both electric and contact, and the attacking vessels were "propelled" or rather guided to the required points by mackerel lines by which they were towed to their doom. The spectacular effect was quite good. These "childish things" have interest in view of the part he was to play later—the last Act—in the attack on the forts in the Narrows of the Dardanelles.

On 12 November 1903 he was appointed to H.M.S. *Albemarle*, Battleship, Captain A. M. Duff, flying the flag ot Rear-Admiral Sir Richard Poore, Bart., one of the Channel Fleet.

During the winter ot 1904-5 the *Albemarle* was in the Mediterrean, and Verner was able to join his father at Gibraltar and go with him to his shooting quarters in Spain. Verner was a very keen sportsman, and he always reckoned one of the whitest of his life the day on this trip, when his father posted him in a shelter on a promontory

1905

with his 8-bore single gun and rode off to "drive" the wildfowl in the surrounding lagunas. Nor where the results bad, Verner shot three Grey Lag Geese, two Wild Duck and five Wigeon, all high driving shots down-wind. The joy of such a day can be realised only by those who know what wild shooting means.

In August 1905 a British Fleet under Admiral Sir Arthur Knyvet Wilson was sent on a cruise to the North Sea and Baltic. Among the places visited were Swinemünde, (Kiel) and Neufahrwasser (Danzig), and the interest of the trip received a decided fillip from the thinly veiled vexation of the Kaiser and the Germans in general at the appearance of our ships in what they considered to be their own "preserved" waters. Verner had his father as his guest in the *Albemarle* on this cruise, and some amusement was caused by the pertinacity with which the German officers and others sought to find out the object of his voyage, for to them it was unthinkable that a Military Staff Officer could possibly go to sea with his son in a battleship, save in furtherance of some deep laid scheme.

In November 1905 upon Captain Duff leaving the *Albemarle* he certified Verner as " an able and zealous officer, who has keenly interested himself in the Gunnery work of the ship."

1906. Verner left the *Albemarle* in January 1906 and in March he was appointed to H.M.S. *Excellent* (the official name for the Gunnery School at Whale Island) to qualify as Gunnery Lieutenant and, during the manœuvres of that year, served in H.M.S. *Spartiate*.
1907. Upon the termination of the Long Course for Gunnery Lieutenants in April 1907 he was placed on the Junior Staff at Whale Island, going in August to the Royal Naval College,
1908. Greenwich, for the Greenwich Course, and returning in July 1908 to Whale Island, where
1909. he served on the Junior Staff until August 1909. By this experience he became an excellent lecturer and teacher, clear in exposition and interesting in manner, which enabled him to hold the attention of his class. Especially he developed a good lecturing style, easy and at the same time arresting. He was not without literary aptitude, which enabled him to give form to his lectures. They were not at all the bald shapeless stuff so often dumped down before unfortunate "students" and called a Lecture. Verner was also helped by his insight into human nature, especially young human nature; he could sympathize with those whom he was teaching, as he could with those who served under him. All this made his lectures human.

On 10 August 1909 he was appointed 1st Lieutenant and Gunnery Lieutenant of H.M.S. *Juno*, 2nd Class Cruiser, 5,600 tons, and so was now in a position to show

A DRIVE AFTER WILD GEESE IN SOUTHERN SPAIN, 1905.

his qualities; and Captain H. T. Millar's certificate ("a most efficient and smart Gunnery Officer, and has performed his duties as First Lieutenant in a very creditable manner") shows the impression he had made.

On 15 December 1910 he went to the Royal Naval Barracks, Portsmouth (H.M.S. *Victory*), Commodore A. M. Duff, under whom he had served in the *Albemarle*. Here he remained until May 1912. During these seventeen months his work was largely disciplinarian. From time to time there is a serious congestion of men in these barracks and to keep order is not always the simplest matter. But Verner knew how to handle men, and boys too. He was strict, and did not spare; but the men knew he was fond of them and took an interest in them; so they took his vigorous language cheerfully and there was no trouble. In short he was a friend to his men and they knew it. As one of them said to Verner's father after his death: "We would have all gone to hell for our Commander." A remarkable instance of what he could do with men occurred in 1911. Stokers, as every one knows, are not considered the easiest of men to manage, especially when ashore. However, Verner believed they could be got into shape like other men, if rightly handled; so he undertook to turn out a first-rate team of stokers for the Royal Naval and Military Tournament. He took them in hand himself and trained them with great care "on his own lines." His special theory was that every one was to be personally responsible for some one thing and "*never to let go of it*." The result surprised the Navy and was something of a shock to H.M.S. *Excellent*. Verner's stokers won, beating the picked guns' crews from Portsmouth, Plymouth and Chatham; and the Shield left Whale Island for the very last destination dreamt of. This was the first occasion on which a team of stokers competed at the Tournament.

The Commodore (A. M. Duff) says in his certificate dated 2 October 1911 "I would be very glad to have him as Gunnery Officer in any ship I commanded."

On 23 May 1912 Verner was appointed Gunnery Lieutenant to H.M.S. *Inflexible*, Battle Cruiser, 17,250 tons, Captain A. J. Phipps Hornby. Verner had now reached a most important point in his career, to which his natural bent, even his amusements, and all his recent training had tended. Gunnery was to be his great work. Gunnery naturally appealed to an intellectual man with a mathematical turn of mind. He was always thinking out gunnery problems. His little book* shows the trend of his mind.

38 Memoir

1912. After a few months cruising to Norway and Denmark the *Inflexible* was re-commissioned at Chatham on 5 November 1912 as part of the Battle Cruiser Squadron in the Mediterranean—Captain Arthur N. Loxley (who went down in the *Formidable* on 1 January 1915)—being Admiral Sir A. Berkeley Milne's Flagship.

1913. In the following spring the *Inflexible* was with the International Fleet which had been assembled in the Near East in view of the Balkan War, and subsequently made a demonstration off Montenegro, whose Government was not inclined to obey the Powers' orders to give up Scutari. In April 1913 the King of Greece was assassinated and the various constituents of the International Fleet sent parties to represent their respective countries at the funeral in Athens. Verner was with the British party. A little incident just before the funeral has especial point in view of our subsequent struggle with the Germans. Verner describes it in a letter to his father (from Malta, 14 April 1913).

. . . "We have been to Athens for the Funeral. The International Fleet landed about 800 seamen and there was *no entente.*

We went up with the Germans and on arrival at the station, whence the coffin was *going*, we found that *they* had a very good billet evidently by previous arrangement whilst we had the very worst possible.†

This could not be allowed and so we took up the position shown in red.

A little Greek Staff Officer explained that that position was allotted to Greek Infantry and that we must go to the position I have shown.

We said, if he wanted room for the Greek Army he would have to huck the Germans out of their position as we weren't going to be placed second to any one!

We had a two hour wrangle in the midst of which the Greeks arrived behind us and things looked rather desperate; however they finally turned about and we saw them no more.

---

* "Guns and Projectiles," by Rudolf H. C. Verner, Lieutenant-Commander, Royal Navy. Published by Gieve, The Hard, Portsmouth, 1914. Second Edition, 1917.

† It will be seen by the sketch on the opposite page that the British detachment was posted in the position usually allotted to a "junior corps," namely on the *left* of the line of quarter-columns. Further it had been so arranged that upon the Greek detachment taking up their assigned position, the British detachment would have been hidden from the view of all those taking part in the ceremony. Hence the description of the "billet" as "the very worst possible." Prince Henry of Prussia (the Kaiser's brother) who was present, was credited with this arrangement.

It is of some interest to note that the four powers shown in the "line of quarter-columns" on the right of the sketch were, less than eighteen months later, fighting as allies against the Germans opposite to them.—ED.

Prince Henry of Prussia Outwitted

Ours was a good place since we became a Guard of Honour being in front of where the coffin was carried into the station. . . .

. . . Prince Henry was dam sick and there *may* be questions raised. Evasive answer!"

In fact there were no questions asked in Parliament, so evasive answers were not needed. No doubt the German Government was more than content to let the incident pass unnoticed.

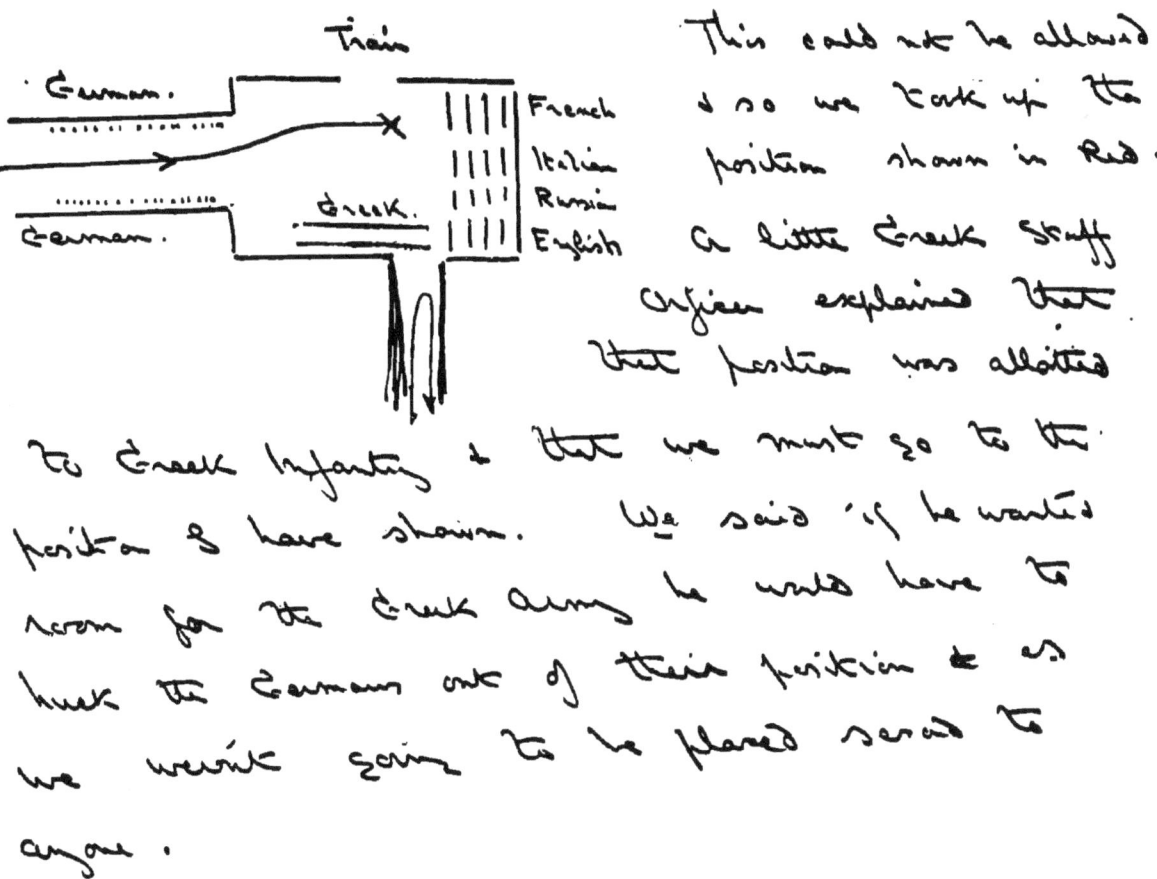

In the following May the First Lord of the Admiralty (then Mr. Winston Churchill) visited the Mediterranean Fleet and saw some firing practice. Lieutenant Verner, as Gunnery Officer of the Flagship, was able to direct the First Lord's attention to the question of opening fire with heavy guns at extremely long ranges, a matter which had especially exercised the minds of the younger school of gunnery officers. He writes to his father from Malta 29 May 1913:—

1913.   ... "Had a busy and interesting week with W(inston) C(hurchill). On the 21st we went out for Squadron Firing, Full Charges, Shell, etc. Owing to a misprint we fired at 6,000 yards, we had meant to fire at 7,000.

He (W. C.) asked me about the shoot, etc., and I told him the range was much too close, but that as some of the ships had 6-inch we had decided on a short-range shoot.

He said: 'What would *you* shoot at?'

I replied: '12,000 yards on a fine day.'

'What about the 9·2 and 6-inch?'

I said: 'Because a pistol will not hit a man at 500 yards, one does not refrain from using a rifle, if one has one. In effect, open fire with 12-inch at long range and then bring 9·2 and 6-inch into action as you close.'

This occurred on a Friday. He *was* leaving on Saturday, but *that* morning orders came for a Special Firing to take place on the Monday in three Phases.

1st, 12,000 yards, 12-inch guns.

2nd, 9,000 yards, 12 and 9·2-inch guns.

3rd, 6,000 yards, 12, 9·2 and 6-inch guns.

A good allowance of ammunition was granted (all extra). This ship got 32 full charges.

On Monday the firing took place and was d—d bad. *I* opened fire at 13,600 yards and fired for four minutes till the range was 12,100 yards, 20 rounds and 2 or 3 hits. Everyone most impressed with this ship's shooting. W. C. and Admiral delighted, etc. As a matter of fact, our shoot was *fair*. Anyhow it is a great triumph for me to have *caused* such a shoot to take place.

I have never fired over 9,000 yards before, nor ever seen it."

Later in the year (10 August 1913) he writes on another gunnery question of great importance:—

"On our last cruise we did a good deal of firing. One night we went out for our annual night-firing test. Groups of moored targets which have to be found by search-light and fired on for a limited time.

We are allowed 200 rounds of 4-inch for this practice and it seldom happens that a ship fires *half* of this.

We were given the usual order, 'ammunition unlimited,' and I issued 270 rounds of which we fired 262 in *four minutes*, range 2,500 to 1,500 yards and got about 70 hits!

H—l of a row now as to how to account for expenditure of ammunition.

I warned 'em that I should be able to fire well over 200 rounds, but they, the 'Starf,' knew better!"

The annual Battle Practice was carried out near Gibraltar in the following November and the *Inflexible* won the Cup with some very good shooting, gaining the warm praise of the Admiralty officials present.

First Intimation of War

On 1 January 1914 the First Lieutenant of the *Inflexible* received promotion and Verner was appointed "First and Gunnery Lieutenant." Having over eight years service as Lieutenant he bore the rank of Lieutenant-Commander. He was now in his thirty-first year.

In the course of the usual Mediterranean cruises during the next few months the *Inflexible* in July visited Constantinople, when the Sultan treated the Ship's Company to a large present of Turkish sweetmeats. In the light of subsequent events this seems something of an irony; as Verner wrote in a letter to his father in the following March, during the bombardment of the Dardanelles.

"Taking in ammunition the night after a day's firing I stopped on the main deck and asked how many more Lyddite were to go down. One was being lowered at the moment and fouling one of the lower hatches hung up there. Voice from below, ''Ere! Steady on with that bit of Turkish Delight.'"

It was on Thursday 30 July 1914 when on her way under orders for home between Alexandria and Malta that the *Inflexible* received the first intimation of war. Here is Verner's log:

"Sent for 1 a.m. by Captain who told me we had received the Warning Telegram."

Henceforward his life may be summed up in three episodes: the pursuit of the *Goeben*; the battle of the Falkland Islands; and the Dardanelles. It is remarkable that his ship was fighting from the very beginning. He regarded this, of course, as splendid luck; as indeed he regarded his coming in for the war at all.

"It *is* glorious, Dad, *whatever* happens," he said a few weeks later, when parting from his father at Plymouth, on his way to the Falklands.

On 3 August his father wrote to Verner as follows:—

"Hartford Bridge,
Winchfield,
3 August 1914.

My Dear Dodo,—This afternoon we were at Tylney and Lionel Phillips telephoned up to town and got the message that England had declared war and was sending an Expeditionary Force.

It is tremendous news, but it is right and proper we should do so. Had England waited she would have been charged with deserting her friends. Bob has joined the *Grafton* at Pompey. We know no more. I attach great importance to keeping Italy neutral. If only she would attack Austria! Anyway, Italy neutral gives France two or perhaps four more Corps to use against Germany.

You can imagine my feelings at being unable to take the field. It is the first time for forty years I have not been ready for it. Alas!

However I have you to take my place and I feel you will do it right well.

God bless you my dear boy. Remember! 'No Surrender!'*

Ever your affte. father,
WILLOUGHBY VERNER."

Upon hearing of the warning from the Captain Verner proceeded to get the fighting equipment of the ship, so far as his duties were concerned, into complete war trim. "Got up 200 lyddite and charges for the eight superstructure guns, etc." is the entry on this day. On the next, "Preparing for battle, fused 4in. lyddite (600). Painted out all bright work and commenced stripping cabins of woodwork, etc. Landed wood gear, gratings, pictures, furniture, etc." "All arrangements," he says on 3 August, "have gone very smoothly, the men knowing their stations and duties in a way very satisfactory to me. There is rather an apathetic feeling aboard since we do not know whom we are going to fight or for what reason."

Something of Verner's character can be seen from a little tussle he had with the Naval Ordnance Authorities at Malta.

"'They had,' he says, 'refused to supply me with the Mark V. (latest Electric tube) on the grounds that such were only to be used for Battle Practice and Gun-layers Test. God help 'em! Saw Chief of Staff; 1,500 tubes arrived at 6 p.m.

4 August (Tuesday) Heard at noon that *Goeben* and *Breslau* had bombarded Philippeville, that *Indefatigable* and *Indomitable* had met them near there and that they were all four returning this way. Poor luck that war is not declared since our two Battle Cruisers should have settled the pair. At 6 p.m. heard that the German cruisers had outpaced ours (they are newer and supposed to possess a couple of knots more speed) and that they were making for Messina, which the Italians are apparently allowing them to use as a base.

8 p.m. Received telegram to the effect that hostilities were to be commenced against Germany at midnight, Italy remaining neutral. This I apprehend means no trouble from Austria, since she will not risk any reduction of fighting power on sea whilst Italy preserves her strength. 10 p.m. *Dublin* lost sight of *Goeben* and *Breslau* steaming East. The *Gloucester* is near Messina to report if they come through. Fine moonlight night.

5 August (Wednesday) 9.30 a.m. Sighted the topmasts of *Indefatigable* and *Indomitable* who met us at 11 a.m. Capt. Kennedy of *Indomitable* came on board. He spent a most anxious day yesterday, since he was ordered to keep touch of the *Goeben* at all costs and when she began to draw away in the afternoon it must have been an awful temptation to stop her. Lord knows when we shall get another such chance at her. She has the heels of everything on the Station and will probably be responsible for enormous losses to commerce.

* The Rallying Cry of Loyal Ulstermen, dating from the Siege of Derry.

The Goeben and Breslau

Noon. Set course for Bizerta, 15 knots. *Indomitable* is going to coal there and we remain somewhere south of Sardinia to cover the transport of the Algerian Army Corps across to France against attack of *Goeben*.

6 p.m. Entered Bizerta Roads. *Indomitable* parted company to coal and we went out to take up our patrol line to the S. of Sardinia. It is thought that there is a bare possibility of the *Goeben* breaking through to the west at dawn.

Steam for full-speed ordered at 4 a.m. Owing to the full moon and great visibility we manned all 12in. guns, keeping four 4in. gun's crews closed up in case of an accidental collision with the French flotilla.

Up at 3.50 a.m. No news. Daylight at 5.10. Nothing in sight save the masts and funnels of *Chatham* and *Weymouth*, hull-down on the eastern horizon; have been steaming slowly east towards Maritima in hopes of meeting our *friends*. No news from Messina save that both ships were there last night and that the Italian authorities are taking steps to move them. Can get no information from the French Admiral as to his dispositions in case *Goeben* goes north —about Corsica.

5 p.m. The 2nd French Battle Squadron left with seven transports this morning. *Dublin* and two T.B.D.'s have been sent to reinforce the R(ear) A(dmiral)* *Defence*, who is still off the entrance to the Adriatic.

7 p.m. *Gloucester* reports *Goeben* and *Breslau* leaving Messina and steering east. We are heading for the Malta Channel at ten knots and there is a chance that during the night *Dublin* and the two T.B.D.'s now off Syracuse and R.A. with four Cruisers and eight T.B.D.'s may get a chance.

Up at 4.15. Very fine morning. Hear that *Defence* and Cruisers have missed a fine chance *seemingly* due to a mutual objection of all concerned to force an action. *Gloucester* remained in touch right through the day and up to 5 p.m. when she was re-called in order to coal. Before turning back she engaged *Breslau* at long range until *Goeben* turned back to assist her consort.

We entered harbour, Valletta, at 12.30 and coaled. Not very much news to be had in Malta. A mass of rumour, of course to the advantage of us and our Allies."

On this day he wrote to his father the following letter:—

" H.M.S. *Inflexible*,
Mediterranean Fleet,
7 August 1914.

DEAR DAD,—Here we are again just going into Malta to coal. We left on Tuesday (4th) and received the order to commence hostilities that night. The *Goeben* is our special job and we have been busy keeping her to the East (away from the French transports). So far, we (*Inflexible*) have not seen her, but *Indefat.* and *Indom.* remained with her all Tuesday and could do nought. We looked into Bizerta on Wednesday to obtain information as to French affairs. All last night and at present *Goeben* has been steaming towards Matapan with two cruisers, *Gloucester* and *Dublin*, commanded by the brothers Kelly, watching her. I think there is little doubt she is going to sit on the trade route off Port Said. On

---

* Rear-Admiral Ernest Troubridge.

1914. Wednesday we captured her collier, 6,000 tons of best Welsh coal ordered to Jedda. This may prove a great help to us. I will finish this on arrival.

10.30 p.m. Finished coaling and leave to-night midnight. Had hoped to hear from you, but the mails are, very naturally, all to blazes.

V. Falzon, tailor, Valletta, has all my papers, guns, etc. I told you this in my last letter and only repeat it in case the letter does not reach you. . . . Think of the luck of the family! 110 years since the last business, since which the fighting man has been considered as rather a contemptible creature by the *superior* money-making swine *who are now snivelling* and I now find myself in a position which *governs* the fortune of the ship in battle and whate'er befalls cannot be but gratifying to you and me.

Your loving son,
Dodo."

Verner's log continues :—

8 August (Saturday)

"6 p.m. Left harbour at 12.30 a.m.; ship darkened. To-night defence stations when outside. Shaped course for Matapan, fifteen knots. *Goeben* is supposed to be somewhere off San Gorgio (at least *I* think that is where she ought to be since it governs the Black Sea—Gibraltar and Athens—Egypt lines). Passed a French cargo boat who have been spoken by *Goeben* early this morning. It is strangely un-German not to have sunk her. Received an order to commence hostilities against Austria and what the devil *we* are to do is hard to say. I imagine that this has arisen as a result of conversations between *Rome* and London. Altered course N. ten knots, and ordered R(ear) A(dmiral)'s Squadron to come south. This, I fear, will leave *Goeben* very much too free a hand in the Levant, but till the French get their squadron East, we *cannot* do aught but keep together.

At 4 p.m. the above signal was cancelled but we still held to our northerly course.

9 August (Sunday)

An uneventful night. Up at 3.45. No news. Ordinary routine with stand-up church. Hymn for peace sung. D——d discreditable, *I* think. *We* should only pray for peace when there is nothing left to fight. P.M. Received orders from home to chase *Goeben*, so off to the East via Matapan. *Indefatigable* and *Indomitable* in company, and two light cruisers should arrive to-morrow forenoon. The R.A. remains with T.B.D.'s to watch against *Goeben* trying to enter the Adriatic."

It will be noticed that up till noon (9 August 1914) the *Inflexible* had received no orders to pursue the *Goeben* and so was precluded from making any attempt to catch her when there was best chance of succeeding.

10 August (Monday)

"As there seemed no chance of meeting with hostile destroyers we went to action stations at 7 p.m. (last night) keeping only four 4-inch manned. Nothing happened during the night and at 4 a.m. we rounded Cape Malia,* and spread fifteen miles, on a N.E. search line.

At 10 a.m. we were startled by intercepting a wireless signal, force 12, i.e., maximum intensity, and evidently originating from a high-power installation close to us (? *Goeben*). Raised steam for full-speed and hoped for the best. Sent the *Weymouth* on to search the Islands to the north and east of the Gulf of Athens. 5 p.m. Action stations as for Monday night.

* Southern point of Greece, east of Cape Matapan.

The Goeben gets off

In the early morning *Weymouth* looked into Syra. Blowing hard from the north and a fair sea running. At 11 a.m. came news that *Goeben* was off the Dardanelles at 9 p.m. 10th. Sent *Weymouth* on at full speed to find out whilst we three Battle Cruisers on a fifteen-mile front patrolled slowly northward.   *1914 11 August (Tuesday)*

At 4 p.m. a report from *Weymouth* that she had attempted to enter the Dardanelles but had been stopped.

We are now pushing on at twenty knots to investigate and should be off the entrance at midnight.

Noon. The worst has happened. After spending a wakeful night, two turrets fully manned and awake, hoping to get a sight of our friends, we received a report from *Weymouth* at 10 a.m. that:—   *12 August (Wednesday)*

> '*Goeben* and *Breslau* passed through Chanak at 10 o'clock last night and are now at Constantinople, *sold to the Turks and re-named*.'

The whole show is so fantastic that it is difficult to believe in its reality. Two modern untouched German ships selling themselves to a *Neutral* power within a week of hostilities commencing! We now await confirmation of our intelligence from England and further orders.

In a way it is, of course, very satisfactory to have moved two potentially dangerous ships from the board without loss to ourselves; but at the same it is very mortifying to *us* concerned. The Ward Room was rather a comic sight this morning. We had just finished our morning 'Action Stations' when the news arrived, and the sight of the 'Control' and 'Quarters'' Officers sitting dejectedly about the room made one think of the Lions' House at feeding time and a butchers' strike just announced."

Such was the lame and impotent conclusion of the pursuit of the *Goeben*. Much, maybe, yet remains to say about it; it is certain the last word has not been said. Admiral Berkeley Milne, at any rate, cannot be blamed in the matter. He was not given a chance by the Authorities until it was too late. No doubt they had to think of the safe crossing of the French transports from Africa; but meantime the *Goeben* was getting away. The next entry in Verner's journal runs:—

"Noon. Patrolled up and down off Lemnos till dawn. The Greeks were there working a search-light, evidently anxious as to the next move of Turkey. Spoke a *Messageries* boat which told us that on Wednesday morning she was boarded at Chanak by an officer from the *Goeben* who threatened to sink the ship if she did not dismantle her wireless.   *13 August (Thursday)*

At 3 a.m. received orders to commence hostilities against Austria. Accordingly proceeded south, 20 knots, for Malta in company with two light cruisers. Left the *Indomitable* and *Indefatigable* to watch the Dardanelles in case our prey comes out and sent a light cruiser to Port Said.   *14 August (Friday)*

At 10 p.m. last night insult was heaped on injury by an order to prepare small targets for aiming practice to-day!

**1914
15 August
(Saturday)**

Secured in Grand Harbour 5 p.m. Commenced coaling 6 p.m. finished 1 a.m., took in 1,680 tons and 100 oil. This morning cleaning ship and sleeping P.M.

Full of rumours *re* fighting in the North Sea, all of which are difficult to believe. I cannot conceive the big fleets meeting at present unless the Expeditionary Force has become a magnet. Meanwhile we await here, waiting, I imagine, to see what Turkey proposes to do with her German ships.

16 August (Sunday)

Received orders last night to draw all the gear landed when we prepared for battle and to go to Plymouth. I imagine that we shall then join up with one of the Cruiser Squadrons at home.

17 August (Monday)

Drawing all boats, furniture, &c. Got all my personal effects on board, guns, &c."

On the 18th the *Inflexible* left for Plymouth. She reached Gibraltar on the 21st at 6 a.m. leaving at 3.30 p.m. Passing the Spanish shore, Verner notes (his parents and his home always in his mind) that he " caught a glimpse of El Aguila," his father's house at Algeciras. In the Bay of Trafalgar he notes: " 5 p.m. Off the Retin Hills," below which lay his father's shooting quarters near the Laguna de la Janda, where he had shot wildfowl and snipe with him in previous years. The ship arrived at Plymouth on Monday 24 August. The Admiral made a farewell speech on Sunday and left at 2 p.m. the next day, " very pleasant."

Verner notes in his diary on arrival:—

24 August (Monday)

" Just had orders to *keep* Admiral's flag flying, which *looks* as though they were doing what I always thought *should* be done—make him Admiral of the Atlantic in charge of trade routes."

Had this been done, there would have been some large ships in the West and the Coronel disaster might never have happened.

All doubts were however dispelled when on the 28th the Admiral struck his flag. Verner's entry in his log on this day is worthy of note, for it expresses the view of those who were in a position to judge recent events.

" The Admiral has had d—d bad luck in having to haul down his flag at such a time. Of course the World will think it is an expression of disapproval by the Admiralty at our having failed to catch the *Goeben*. As a matter of fact such was not our *duty* until too late. To be censured for failing to do what you were neither *ordered* to or *could* do, is rough."

The 28 August he marks thus: " A sad day. Our Captain A. L. Loxley left us." The sadness is accentuated when one thinks that within a few months both Captain Loxley and Verner were dead. Capt. Loxley greatly valued Rudolf Verner and in his certificate he said " I have the highest opinion of him both as a Seaman and a Gunnery Officer. He is an excellent organizer, works hard, and no detail escapes him. Strongly recommended for advancement."

Patrolling the North Sea

Captain Richard Phillimore succeeded Captain Loxley and the *Inflexible* was sent to the North Sea, joining the Grand Fleet at Scapa Flow on 30 August. His entry on the 31st runs "Scapa is indeed a very wonderful sight. Some 60 pennants and over 100 colliers, store ships, &c. Two seaplanes were flying overhead when we entered yesterday."

1914 30 August

The fact that the *Inflexible* was at Scapa Flow was of course not known at this time to the public. Verner was not an ornithologist like his father but he took a keen, and ever keener interest in wild birds, and they had made several cruises together in warships in the North Sea and Baltic. This observation of birds now gave him an opportunity, without infringing any regulations, of making it easy for his father to form a shrewd opinion of the whereabouts of the *Inflexible*. Choughs nesting on the cliffs of the north coast of Ireland, Great Northen Divers frequenting the seas near Scapa Flow, Ruffs and Reeves appearing on the shores of Jutland or flocks of Scoters in the Bight of Heligoland, all mere items of daily observation of the presence of these birds, thus meant much to the receiver of his letters.

For two months the *Inflexible* took part in the North Sea routine, a life of continual care and tense vigilance, hard and at the same time monotonous; altogether a trying ordeal, especially for men who had been serving in very hot latitudes (the summer of 1914 had been exceptionally hot in the Levant) and who now naturally felt the cold of the North Sea.

Now and again a short entry in his journal shows how incessant was the strain and how ever ready were our sailors to meet the enemy. Thus on 31 August we read:—

"Sailed (from Scapa) at 4 p.m. in company, *Lion*, *Princess Royal* and *Queen Mary* (the Cat Class). We feel quite small folk in comparison with these big ships.

31 August

Action sounded off at 3.15 a.m. False alarm. Our own 6th Cruiser Squadron. Ship's Company were at Action Stations within ten minutes of the alarm. Turrets, etc., ready to open fire in five minutes."

1 September

Then follow weeks of patrolling, sometimes "down Norway coast," "N.W. of Shetlands," then "N.W. of Skaw," "near Heligoland," etc., with every possible variety of bad weather and heavy seas logged. Thus on 27 September: "Very uncomfortable night. Reached as far north as 63° 40′, too far this weather and season." Iceland it may be remarked is in latitude 63° 40′ north.

27 September

"Submarines reported in Scapa. People seemed *surprised* at the submarines getting so far from home. *I* think they have shown an extraordinary lack of enterprise in not having done so sooner.

17 October

48 Memoir

1914
21 October

Trafalgar Day. Landed for the first time since Plymouth when I drove to and from station to meet W. V."

That eternal waiting for the enemy did not suit Verner at all, as his letters home at this time bear witness. "Glad you shot well," he says to his father, who had been partridge-driving lately. "Wish to God *I* could get something to shoot at. Here we are: ten weeks of war, 14,000 miles, 11,000 tons of coal and not a *sight* of the blighters!" But the activity of his mind always helped him through a dull phase. He varied the monotony this time by working out an anti-aircraft gun-mounting; for the *Inflexible* was built before danger from enemy air-craft had been considered. "Started work converting one of the 4-inch on 'X' turret to high-angle firing. That one on 'A' is a success." This he completed and, after firing with effect at 5,000 yards, sent in an Official report; which does not seem to have carried conviction; for on 30 October he says: "Have had a snuffy reply: 'Considered unsatisfactory and dangerous.' I want the Captain to reply that it would be a dam sight more unsatisfactory and dangerous to have a blasted fellow overhead whom you could not dislodge. On the other hand —— (at Admiralty) thinks the show satisfactory. *Of course* only a stop-gap until proper mountings are available."

It must be remembered that in these early days of the war only the more modern of our ships were provided with an effective anti-aircraft gun and that it was some time before a satisfactory mounting was supplied to ships built at an earlier date.

Early in November came the news of the destruction of Rear-Admiral Sir Christopher Cradock's squadron off Coronel in Chili. The German Admiral in the Pacific, Graf von Spee, commanded a much more powerful force, including the *Scharnhorst* and her sister ship the *Gneisenau* with some smaller cruisers. The *Scharnhorst* and *Gneisenau* were the best two shooting ships in the German Navy, and had won in succession, in the two preceding years, the Kaiser's medal for shooting. The *Good Hope* and the *Monmouth* after a gallant but hopeless fight were sunk. Thereupon the Admiralty decided to send out Vice-Admiral Sir C. Doveton Sturdee in the *Invincible*, with her sister ship the *Inflexible*, to deal with von Spee's squadron, and the second, the greatest, chapter in Rudolf Verner's fighting career began.

His journal for Thursday 5 November (the ship was at Cromarty) contains this entry:—

Off to the Falklands

"Orders to proceed to Plymouth with *Invincible* and prepare for foreign service. Tropics. Presume we are after Pacific squadron which is reported off Valparaiso. Sailed at 7 p.m.

Arrived at the Sound 8 a.m."

1914
5 November

8 November
(Sunday)

He went up to town on the following Tuesday the 12th and when he and his father were lunching at the United Service Club they met his prospective Admiral, Sir Doveton Sturdee, an old friend. The *Inflexible* sailed at 7 p.m. the next day. The voyage out had not many incidents. St. Vincent was made by 5 p.m. on 17th, the ship leaving again at 6 p.m. the next day.

17 November

"At 7 p.m. stopped engines and buried a boy who was killed at 3 a.m. during coaling. He was tending a whip and was taken round the drum of the electric motor; killed instantanously. I saw him five seconds after it happened and helped to clear him. An impressive ceremony. Ship darkened save for lights for Band and Chaplain. Escort fired three very good volleys."

This is a reminder of the constant danger in which the Naval man lives, whether in peace or in war. He is always fighting; for if there is no enemy, there are the elements, and risks of accident innumerable.

"Hear that Admiral Sturdee is C.-in-C. of S.E. coast, etc. We shall have some ten ships with us and hope to round up *Scharnhorst* and Co. Bound for a reef off the Brazil coast where we hope to find colliers.

19 November
(Tuesday)

At dawn off Roca Isles, where we hoped to find *Karlsrühe* or traces of her. No luck. Set course south towards Monte Video.

23 November
(Monday)

At 7 a.m. made the Abrolhos Reef and Islands; such a quaint sight—two small islands apparently without any vegetation save a solitary row of stunted *pine*-trees (?). A lighthouse and detached building. Here there is also a wireless station with German operator. Two men and five women the total of inhabitants, adult. Found here eight colliers; also *Defence, Carnarvon, Cornwall, Kent, Bristol, Glasgow*."

26 November
(Thursday)

From this place he wrote the following letter to his father (received at Algeciras 4 January 1915).

"H.M.S. *Inflexible*,
27.11.14.

27 November

DEAR DAD,—Here we are again. As usual when I write to you I am d—d tired, just finished coaling, 1,800 tons. Temperature 100° in shade, and off again to-morrow.

We have been changing our latitude 6° a day since we last met and it has been trying. Quite a squadron of us here now.

Had much information *re* action off Valparaiso. It was as I *thought*. An English Admiral manœuvred into a *hopeless* position from which he *could* have extricated himself, refused to do so since 'he would rather burst than let a damned scoundrel of a German,' etc.,

50 Memoir

1914 etc.* ... However, to-day week should put us in the latitude of ‡Hartford Bridge [printed upside-down] and if all goes well, another week should see them extermed or interned. Pray God the former.

We are all wonderfully fit considering all and it is quite *pathetic* to meet old-time friends here and see their genuine pleasure at our arrival. Not only because we are a reinforcement but because we bring news, food and drink. Most of them have had no mails since 29 July.

Your loving son,
B. Razil."

As will be seen there is no mention in the above of any place, but the signature pretty plainly indicated that the letter was written somewhere in the latitude of Brazil.

23 November They left the reef at 10 a.m. on 28th (Saturday) and were off Rio (300 miles east of it) in the afternoon of the next day. Here they were delayed, with far-reaching results that appear later, by the *Invincible* fouling her propeller with a towing wire. She and the *Inflexible* had been towing targets for one another. "Fired thirty-two full charge rounds from 12-inch. First since 1913. Very good results. Accuracy of guns excellent." The squadron finally got away at 3.30 p.m. on 1 December (Tuesday); by which time the *Invincible* was ready to go on. The entry on this day is:—

7 December (Monday) "On 7 December the squadron reached the Falkland Islands. Spent the day analysing fall of shot and plotting same on *Scharnhorst*. Gave us 12—16 hits.

Off Eastern Islands at 6 a.m. Entered harbour 9 o'clock. A desolate land. Found here three colliers. *Glasgow, Carnarvon* and *Bristol* to coal first. We, guardship till 8 a.m. to-morrow. Prepared for coaling.

8 December (Tuesday) Collier alongside at 6 a.m. Commenced coaling. At 8.30 a.m. report from Signal Stations :—

'Strange men-of-war in sight.'

Resumed coaling till 9 a.m. when *Canopus*, in inner harbour, fired two rounds of 12 inch. All this time raising steam. Cast off collier and went to Action Stations. Damned unpleasant. Selected marks for *indirect* firing since the guns could not see the enemy for the land.

From the top a grand view of them. Two advance cruisers and three far distant. At 9.45 under weigh and out of the harbour. A great relief. Enemy then running.

At 12.57 opened fire 16,000 yards on *Leipzig*. Armoured cruisers *Scharnhorst* and *Gneisenau* turned to port and we and *Invincible* engaged them.

---

* A paraphrase of Nelson's famous words to Colonel the Hon. William Stewart of the 95th Rifles (now Rifle Brigade) :—'For myself, I would rather burst than let a dammed rascal of a Frenchman know that peace or war affected me with either joy or sorrow.'—*Cumloden Papers*, described in the *History of the Rifle Brigade*, Part I, p. 65.

‡ Hartford Bridge, Winchfield, Hants, his home in England, is roughly in latitude 51 degrees North that of Cape Horn is in latitude 51 degrees South. Hence the inversion of 'Hartford Bridge.'

Action of Falkland Islands

Small cruisers scattered, followed by our other ships. Action till 2 p.m. inconclusive.

Re-engaged at 3 p.m. and at 4 p.m. sank *Scharnhorst*. Desultory action from 4.5; we practically out of action due to *Invincible* smoke.

Finally *left* her and ran the show ourselves, quickly disabling *Gneisenau* who sank at 6 p.m. Picked up nine officers and fifty-five men.

Little damage. One shell on fore-turret; one, main derrick. One man killed.

Heard that *Nürnberg* had been sunk by *Kent* and *Leipzig* by *Cornwall* and *Glasgow*. *Bristol* sank two colliers. Chasing *Dresden*."

After searching the bays and inlets in Tierra del Fuego ("the most desolate coast I have ever *dreamt* about") they made for the western entrance of the Straits of Magellan, having received orders to search till 29th and then return to England via Falkland Islands, Abrohlos, and St. Vincent. But on the 18th they suddenly received new orders that Battle Cruisers were wanted at home and they were to return to Port Stanley to coal and thence to make for St. Vincent. On their way Verner notes (19 December, Sunday): " Wonderful sunset effect on mountain tops fifty miles away. They were snow-covered and had not been visible in full sunlight and as the sun dipped they stood out of the sea like pink icebergs."

They anchored in Port William at 7 a.m. on the 23rd and coaled, leaving again at 11.30 a.m. the next day.

"Rather a muddle at present. Admiralty have ordered us to Gib. Sir F. Sturdee directed us to remain at Falkland Islands and *wait* for him and we know that both cruisers are wanted at home."

On 31st they anchored at Abrolhos at 7.30 a.m., finding the *Canopus* there doing guardship. After taking in 1820 tons of coal they left at 5.30 p.m.

On 1 January (1915) they heard that the *Newcastle* had been in action with the *Dresden* and an armed merchantman.

On 4 January we have the entry "7 p.m. Heard of my promotion." He had been specially promoted to the rank of Commander on 31 December 1914, being still in his 31st year. He was thus in the "first flight."

Very shortly after this Commander Wigram was sent from the *Inflexible* to the *Empress of Britain* as Captain, Verner being appointed Acting-Commander of the *Inflexible* in his place. But he does not refer to this with any satisfaction; on the contrary he says (6 January) "To my great annoyance heard that Wigram is to be sent to *Empress of Britain* as Captain. This will leave me with more than I can *properly* do."

1915

It must be remembered that the duties of Commander of a Battle Cruiser are alone sufficiently strenuous and that he had now to perform these *in addition* to those of Gunnery Officer.

7 January

On 7th they anchored at St. Vincent. "Took in 220 rounds of 12-inch. *Very welcome.*"

It was well that the *Inflexible* had not had to fight on the way back.

On 8th (Friday), Commander Wigram left the ship. "Gave him a good send off." About this time Verner heard of the death of his old Captain and close friend, Captain A. H. Loxley, who went down with his ship, the *Formidable*, near Plymouth on 1 January 1915. Verner had felt parting from him when he left the *Inflexible* very much, as we saw, and now he notes: "Wrote to Mrs. Loxley; very sad. In his old cabin and at his desk."

The ship was then passing the Canaries.

12 January

At 2.15 p.m. on 12 January 1915 she anchored off the New Mole at Gibraltar. By a happy coincidence Verner's father was in Gibraltar that afternoon. He heard of his son's unexpected arrival in a curious way. As he was walking down the main street, a Marine post-man (who knew Colonel Verner from his being on the *Inflexible* as a guest in the cruise to Norway two years before) came up and said "The ship is in, Sir, and Lieutenant Verner has been made our Commander, Sir." The Colonel of course spoke to him, congratulating him on the victory of the Falkland Islands battle. "Yes, Sir," said the man, "and *we* all say, Thanks to Commander Verner." This was, of course, very proper enthusiasm for his ship and his Commander. But there is no doubt that very many of the ship's Company did believe that they owed the victory to their Gunnery Officer! Letters to relations and friends showed this.

So the chapter of the Falkland Islands ended felicitously for Rudolf Verner; a contrast artistically complete to the story of the pursuit of the *Goeben*. He had been a central figure in the most striking Naval incident of the war, and the first decisive Naval action England had fought for over a century. He had had his chance and taken it. To him besides all this it had given an intellectual satisfaction peculiar to himself. For ten years or more he had been constantly thinking and planning to this end. "The thing," he wrote to an intimate friend, "which pleased me most over the Falkland show was that for once at any rate in my life practice proved *my* theories and it all befell as I had expected and worked for." The spirit of this remark might be misunderstood but it was really the artist's satisfaction in achievement—a thing very rarely enjoyed. His account of the Battle, from which his theories can be deduced, is given elsewhere in this book in his own words with his own illustrations, for Rudolf had a good deal of his father's gift for draughtsmanship.

Saturday 16 January was his 32nd birthday, which he was happily able to spend with his own people. "Family to lunch" (in the *Inflexible*) he notes in his diary. Later on he went over to Algeciras and spent that evening and the next day with his father and mother at El Aguila, their delightful Spanish winter-quarters. After this "Rest-Kure," as he calls it, he returned to the ship very early Monday morning.

At 9.30 p.m., after dark, the *Inflexible* left with sealed orders. Next day it appeared that they were to go East, clearly for operations against the Dardanelles.

After a very heavy gale—the biggest sea, he says, he had ever known in the Mediterranean—they neared the Greek Archipelago on 23rd and anchored S.E. of Skyros the next day, where they found the *Indefatigable* and some French men-of-war.

The ship's movements were neatly suggested to his father by the signature "Yours, Archie" to a letter written on the 31st. In this letter he says, "After our recent arduous days we are enjoying quite a quiet life—save myself who have much too much to do; I am not sure how long I can do it." He was still both Gunnery Officer and Acting Commander in place of Commander Wigram who had not yet returned.

Nearly three months earlier, on 4 November, the day before the Battle Cruisers left the North Sea for their dash to the Falklands, he had written to his father:—"Bad luck missing the Dardanelles show"; but that was not to be his luck. However if he could not read his own future, he *could* read the signs of the times. In this letter he said:—"We *ought* to have done it on 12 August," when the *Goeben* and *Breslau* fled into the Dardanelles for shelter and "sold" themselves to Turkey.

Verner saw clearly that both the right time and the right way of doing this job had been missed. He did not admire this expedition and felt that there was want of thought, want of plan, want of preparation.

The next three were busy weeks. Tremendously bad weather delayed coaling for four days. On 3 February it was "blowing a hurricane (force of squalls, 11-12), sleet, hail and snow. Coaling impossible, could not stand on deck owing to force of wind." However on the 5th the weather improved and 1,150 tons were shipped. Later, gravel was taken on board for "feed-tank protection," 20 tons one day and 38 tons on the next.

1 February   Among the gunnery preparations he notes "Under weigh at 8 a.m., sub-calibre firing. Control from below. Very satisfactory."

11 February   "Carried out a very successful calibration against a small rock, 10,000 yards range. Three rounds per gun. Average spread, 70 yards. Actually obtained four hits."

On the 15th he enters in his diary "Cut out a 10-foot silhouette of *Goeben*, primed with ·303 blank cartridges" and on the following day he adds "Aiming rifle-practice in forenoon, *Goeben* looks very life-like."*

18 February   On the 18th Vice-Admiral Carden came on board the *Inflexible*. "Just missed being ordered home. We *were* to have left on the arrival of the Q.E.† but since that ship has broken down (speed fifteen knots) we are to remain as Flagship."

In a letter to Colonel Verner (dated 14 February) he refers to the likelihood of action in a short time.

"Before you receive this we shall have been at it again and very interesting it will be. The element of luck will figure to a great extent so I can make no prophecy.

A wonderful collection of ships gathered from every sea the Navy has flown a flag in. My *first* ship ‡ is with us and some old French friends ∥ I have 'sunk' in some of our naval lake actions. I will write again before we start and will give you details since by *then* there will be no object to censor the letter. Wigram has not yet returned but I hope he will turn up with our reinforcements. Carried out a calibration last week and found the guns *in first class condition*; so much for the 'failure' of the wire gun. At 10,000 yards fired 24 rounds at a rock 20 feet × 15 feet and 10 feet high and got 4 hits and 8 shots within 20 yards of it. Am very fit and keen to get going again but I rather fear that we shall be kept in the background for the first part of the show.

It is funny to be back here in (or nearly in) the place we were when the incident which gave excuse for the war occurred." §

The attack on the Dardanelles began on 19 February (Friday).

19 February   "A beautiful day. Off the entrance to the Dardanelles. A long range and very desultory bombardment. Ships first engaged: *Suffren* and *Gaulois*, *Vengeance* and *Cornwallis*, *Triumph* and ourselves. Fired 24 rounds between 10 and 5 p.m., of which 18 *looked* likely.

---

* It should be explained that the rifles he alludes to here were mounted on the *Inflexible*'s guns and that the dummy *Goeben* target was towed past by a Picket boat at about 200 yards range. The guns were then "trained" on the moving target and the rifles fired at it. When one of the ·303 blank cartridges with which the *Goeben* was "primed" was struck by a bullet, it exploded. This was a very old device of Verner's dating back to his boyhood's naval battles on Sandhurst lake and, later, at Minley Manor.—ED.

† *Queen Elizabeth*.

‡ H.M.S. *Majestic*, sunk subsequently by German submarine attack on 27 May 1915.

∥ The French Battleship *Bouvet*, sunk by floating mine, 18 March 1915.

§ The escape of the *Goeben*.

H.M.S. *INFLEXIBLE* IN ACTION AT THE DARDANELLES.

Firing at Seddul Bahr Fort, 25 February, 1915.

The Attack on the Outer Forts

At 5 p.m. *Vengeance* and *Cornwallis* were ordered to close and attack forts No. 1 and No. 4; and things brightened up at once. *Vengeance* was fired on by No. 4 and ought to have been hit. She herself was busy with No. 1 and never realized this. We fired 21 rounds into No. 1 at 12,000 yards; which ruined the *accuracy* of the fire, if it did not silence the guns. Anyhow both *Vengeance* and *Cornwallis* withdrew without harm."

Thus did Verner briefly describe the day when the British Squadron attacked and silenced the outer forts guarding the entrance to the Dardanelles. The *Inflexible* on this day once again gave proof of her good gunnery, for towards evening fort No. 4 suddenly opened fire on the *Vengeance* and the *Inflexible* came into action at short notice and made excellent practice, firing 19 rounds which greatly disconcerted the Turkish gunners and destroyed the accuracy of their fire.*

20 February (Saturday)
"The morning spent in talk and the afternoon in more talk." Bad weather prevented the renewal of the action until 25th (Thursday).

Referring to the action of the 19th in a letter to his father (dated 24 February) he described it:

"A very pretty sight. I imagine that ashore it would be described as a reconnaissance, but there was plenty of 'force' about. For ourselves, we kept out of harm's way and contented ourselves with stopping those forts which were inclined to annoy the in-shore squadron. Common shell ashore makes a pretty spectacle.

No news of Wigram. A very strenuous life these days, almost peace routine. We are simply full up with officers and men (1,030 victualled).

25 February (Thursday)
Fine day. Took up position for bombardment. We anchored some 11,000 yards from Hellas lighthouse and opened fire on it with my H.A.† gun. (It was reported that the tower was employed for fire-control purposes). Fired 44 rounds and got three hits, two in the building and one in the tower just under the lantern.

Agamemnon anchored 10,000 yards from No. 1 Battery and received nine hits before she could clear away. Lost three killed and eight severely wounded. A distinct misprint. Otherwise the day went well. We put about 15 shell into Seddul Bahr and *Queen Elizabeth* made excellent practice on No. 1.

Vengeance and *Cornwallis* then ran in close and fired point-blank at Nos. 1, 3, 4 and 6 forts: only fired at twice.

Suffren and *Charlemagne* then did a run, the former shooting very well.

The last pair *Triumph* and *Albion* also had a good shoot.

There was no reply but two observation mines exploded near *Albion*.

When we left, at 6 p.m., all forts were in ruins and fires everywhere. Seddul Bahr village had been on fire since the morning and Kum Kale got on fire about 6 p.m.

Sent mine-sweepers up but they found nothing. Returned to anchorage."

* This was specially mentioned by Vice-Admiral Carden in his despatches. (See Appendix II.)
† 'High-angle,' i.e., 'Anti-aircraft.'

1 March (Monday) — Referring to this action, he says writing to his father (1 March):

"At last weather is getting better and we have been able to do a little.

Have broken up forts at entrance and are now starting in on the Narrows which is much bigger game.

Quite a fleet here including my *first* ship, you saw her at Plymouth. So far the Turk has not got his eye in and save for howitzers, which now and then score a hit, have given us little trouble. It is really funny, ships big and small cruising about and suddenly a splash and one tries to guess whom it was meant for.

The next splash is usually either exactly in the same place or so far away that another ship becomes the favourite. Now and then a shrapnel bursts over a ship and every man runs like hell for cover."

On Monday 1 March the Dardanelles Squadron was completed:

"Last of the squadron, the *Majestic* arrived. Fleet now consists of eighteen armoured ships made up of ten different classes.

Still nothing done, though weather better.

2 March (Tuesday) — An attempt was made lately to land 500 Naval Brigade (Antwerp) to cover demolition parties whilst the latter blew up guns in No. 1 and No. 4 forts.

Absolutely fatuous idea. The guns are obviously disabled and can be silenced at once by gunfire if they *are* repaired. Meantime the shore party will probably get a hell of a time. Luckily weather stopped the attempt.

3 March (Wednesday) — Northerly winds caused us to shift over to Imbros for shelter. Another of the curses of the present complete lack of organization is that we have *six* bases! and no one knows where ships are. Consequently 'Operation orders' often arrive on board a ship *after* they should have been carried out.

At 6 p.m. ammunition ships alongside; took in 80 rounds of 12 inch. This brings us up to 878 rounds, 12 inch.

4 March (Thursday) — A bad day. Off the entrance, 10 a.m. Out boats and sent them to assist in the landing parties, 250 each side with demolition parties from this ship and *Lord Nelson*.

Seddul Bahr and Kum Kellassi, the two big forts, in absolute ruins.

Small opposition to the landing parties, but no sooner were the men ashore than they found the Turk ready for them.

The Northern party, with sound sense, abandoned the show and returned with a loss of three killed and three wounded.

The Southern side got involved, asked and received reinforcements and finally had to retire, less nineteen killed, three missing, and twenty-two wounded. Beastly sight seeing wounded men trying to crawl along the beach towards the boats, a mile or so further up the harbour. A T.B.D. put a whaler ashore and got five of them, and we were lucky to get off so lightly. Trust the *Naval* Brigade have had enough of shore operations.

5 March (Friday) — *Queen Elizabeth* moved off the northern side of Gallipoli Peninsula and fired over this into the Narrows forts. Report says that they did well. But the folly and waste of time! The ship did not get her orders till 11 a.m. Then had to get into position, and the best part of daylight had vanished when she began firing. Of course, a field battery opened on her and scored some twenty hits (all ineffective). We stood off at 10,000 yards and shut up the battery with two 4-inch A. A. guns. To-morrow the Turk will have some howitzers ready for the *Q.E.*

Meantime nothing doing inside save that we are slowly collecting hits and casualties.

Wigram* returned. I see a rest cure. *Q.E.* fired one round from her old billet, was shortly afterwards hit by six or eight shell; had to move out 2,000 yards, was hit again and by time she had got to her third position the light had failed. **6 March (Saturday)**

Vengeance was hit twice by 9·4 shell, and at about 10,000 yards; she was inside.

Received a letter from Dorothy telling me of the loss of my old friend."

His brother-in-law, Commander Robert Jeffreys, R.N. was in command of the armed merchant-ship H.M.S. *Clan Macnaughton*, which had recently been lost with all hands while on patrol duty in the North Atlantic. Robert Jeffreys was one of Verner's oldest friends (they had served together in the *Albemarle*)—a fine hard-bitten English sailor, an admirable man, and a good companion—who came to be attached to him yet more closely by his marriage with "Dodo's" only sister, Dorothy. Thus the two friends died for their country very soon one after the other. Commander Jeffreys leaves two sons (with one daughter) to carry on their father's and uncle's Naval tradition.

On 7 March Verner writes :—

"Coaled ship. *I* sat in my cabin, having o to do. **7 March (Sunday)**

Not very encouraging reports from inside. *Agamemnon* was hit eight or nine times by 14-inch and 9·4 inch shell, but no casualties.

Swiftsure and *Triumph* have been down to Smyrna and report a few casualties.

To-morrow *we* are going up, and with luck will get some shooting at the Chanak forts.

Vice-Admiral shifted over to *Q.E.* and went up Dardanelles. As usual, four hours too late, and light was bad. All ships worried by howitzer fire and nothing was effected." **8 March (Monday)**

Soon after this the *Inflexible* went to Malta to "shift over" two fore-turret guns "which wanted a rest."

"At 6 a.m. on the 13th she entered the Harbour and went alongside the wall under the big crane at 7 a.m. Both the guns were shifted by 8 p.m. Went ashore and dined at the Club; practically all old friends gone."

The next day (Sunday) he went to church and later, met a friend, Lord Lucan, an old brother-officer of his father's, at the Malta Club at dinner.

While he was in Malta he wrote to his father for the last time :—

"DEAR DAD,— . . . Poor dear Dorothy. I am too sick at heart to write about it. . .

re Dardanelles. The papers are too hysterical. A ship can always silence a fort *for the time being. Therefore* we could have been at K (Constantinople) a week ago; *but* that would have been useless, unless supplies could reach us.

* Commander Ernest Wigram; he had been away from the ship since 8 January.

Therefore, 150,000 men are required to take and hold the Gallipoli Peninsula, and d——d good men at that!

Met Lord Lucan to-day. Last saw him at Lulworth in 1912 when I landed to play the fool with the Territorials. We arrived *here* yesterday and leave to-morrow.

Re Despatches. S. (Sturdee) informed us of his recommendations and the only one that appeared was *my* hydraulic artificer (D.C. Medal).

'Tis a pity. A *triumph* for me since I have been promoted *despite* it. Everybody seems very pleased with the yarn.* 'The Young Man of Cape Horn' is being well advertised! . . .

This place is a regular French port these days, both afloat and ashore. *Vive l'entente.*

Your loving son,
Dodo."

At 8.30 a.m. on the 15th the *Inflexible* started on her return voyage to the Dardanelles. The only entry in his log on this day was: "Turret ready for action by noon (four days since I dis-classed it.)"

16 March (Tuesday) The fatal day was now drawing near. On Tuesday 16 March he writes: "A beautiful day; off Matapan at noon and since then have been steaming through Greek Islands. Passed a French Squadron of four *Dantons* and five T.B.D.'s, steering west. *Where* have they been? Hear that Ian H. is coming out. Lord help us."

This was the last entry he made in his diary.

17 March (Wednesday) Orders for the attack on the Narrows were issued on the following day 17 March. That evening when he had made all the necessary preparations for the fight, Verner went down to the Ward Room and told his brother officers that they would have a hot time of it on the morrow. At the same time he expressed his determination to go up into the fore-control, in addition to Blaker, as he expected it would be a very difficult matter to direct the fire on the enemy's batteries, which would be firing from three sides. An attempt was made to persuade him to go to the lower control on the grounds that with both officers in the fore-control one shell might take both directors of fire, but he was determined to go to the fore-control for, as he said, he could see better from that point.

The extreme vulnerability of the control position was well known to Verner, for, in addition to his own experiences at the Falklands' action, he knew that the *Kent* had riddled the fore-top of the *Nürnberg* on that day, whilst the *Cornwall* had shot away the fore-topmast of the *Leipzig*, killing the Gunnery Lieutenant and disabling the fore-control.†

* His account of the Falklands' Action.
† "Battle of the Falklands," by Commander H. Spencer Cooper, p. 115.

The Battle of the Narrows

The morning of the 18th was fine with a light southerly wind. At 10.30 the first 18 March (Thursday) line of British ships, consisting of the *Queen Elizabeth*, *Agamemnon*, *Lord Nelson* and *Inflexible*, proceeded up the Straits. They were preceded by a line of Destroyers with sweeps for mines and each ship had a Picket-boat in attendance to deal with floating mines. The *Prince George* on the port-beam of the *Queen Elizabeth* and the *Triumph* on the starboard-beam of the *Inflexible* were intended to deal with the howitzers and field-guns so as to leave the larger ships free to direct their fire undisturbed on the big guns in the Chanak Forts.

By 11 o'clock the ships were engaging howitzers and field-guns firing from the Asiatic shore.

At 11.25 the *Queen Elizabeth* opened fire on a fort and the *Agamemnon*, *Lord Nelson* and *Inflexible* shortly followed suit. The British line was now subjected to a very heavy fire of howitzers and field-guns from concealed batteries. One battery of howitzers, four guns of about 6-in. calibre, was particularly annoying. It was clear to all in the fore-control of the *Inflexible* that they were being made a target for the enemy's fire which was extremely severe ; the ship replying with great precision and vigour.

All the forts, which at this time were 14,000 yards distant, now opened on the ships, but the range made their fire ineffective. Shortly before noon the *Inflexible* silenced a very troublesome enemy gun after firing the third round at it.

About noon the second line, consisting of four French Battleships, came up and, passing the British line, opened on the forts at closer range. The action now became general, both lines, British and French, engaging the forts and detached batteries.

At about 12.20 a shell struck the centre tripod of the foremast of the *Inflexible* and set fire to the fore-bridge and deck-house below. Three minutes later one of the turrets was struck, and almost immediately afterwards the ship received three more hits.

At 12.27 the fore-top was reported "out of action." At the time it was of course unknown whether this meant more than that the instruments or telephones had been disabled, thus severing communication with the guns below.

About 12.40 p.m. the Picket-boat coming up astern of the *Inflexible* was sunk, and a few minutes later the ship received two more hits.

Shortly before 12.30 (the exact time is uncertain, but it was *after* the fore-bridge had been set on fire) a shell struck the fore signal-yard, only a few feet above the fore-control station, and, bursting, sent its fragments downwards perforating the roof and sides of the control and literally plastering it.

At the moment when the fatal shell burst Commander Verner was engaged in "spotting" the effects of the fire with his glasses, both arms up. With him was his assistant Lieutenant Blaker and eight men. Three of the men were killed on the spot and both officers and four out of five remaining men were struck down, only one of the party, A.B. Arthur Robinson, escaping untouched. Owing to the severity of the enemy's fire and the cabins on the fore-bridge immediately below being in flames it was not known to anybody for some time that the control had been struck.

It would seem that the shock of the explosion completely put out of action for some minutes all the survivors in the control. One of the Bluejackets, who himself was very severely wounded, describes how when they recovered from the shock they moved Verner to some mats and " made him as comfortable as possible."

Verner however must have soon recovered enough to get up from the mats he had been laid on and raise himself to the level of the voice-tube, for the Officer in charge of the Fore Transmitting Station received a message through the voice-pipe from Verner to report the " fore-control out of action," adding " we are all dead or dying up here, send up some morphia." The latter part of the message was passed to the Fleet Surgeon who was in the lower Conning Tower next to the Fore Transmitting Station. The Surgeon at once went on deck but was unable to get up to the fore-top as the fire was raging on the bridge and the iron ladder was too hot to climb.

Some time later on, Verner sent down a second message through the voice-pipe saying " For God's sake put out the fire or we shall all be roasted."

With reference to these messages, Lieutenant Leicester Curzon-Howe, the Officer who received them, wrote to Verner's father :—" He spoke to me *twice* through the voice-pipe from the fore-top to the Fore Transmitting Station. He sent down *no other message* except these two and they were sent in an absolutely calm and clear manner and it was not till I got on deck when we were ordered to abandon the Fore Transmitting Station, after striking the mine, that I knew that he himself was so terribly wounded."

As soon as the fire below admitted of it, by Verner's orders those of the survivors who could move helped one another down as best they could. He sent word by one of them to the Captain to " report the fore-control out of action " and to ask the Captain to " go astern," presumably so as to clear the control from the smoke of the funnels. At this time there was a strong breeze blowing direct from the ships towards the Chanak Forts. One of the Bluejackets who was only slightly wounded returned aloft and was sent down by Verner with a message to the Captain to say that he was " unable to carry on."

H.M.S. *INFLEXIBLE* IN THE ATTACK ON THE NARROWS, DARDANELLES,
1.15 p.m., 18 MARCH, 1915.

(*From a painting by Montague Dawson.*)

The Fatal Shell

The situation of those in the fore-top was indeed a desperate one. The cabin on the fore-bridge below and the fore-top itself were on fire and a storm of shells was bursting about the ship.

The Admiral in his despatches mentions that at 12.56 the *Inflexible's* fore-bridge was "blazing fiercely." The crews of the 4-inch guns were at this time engaged in fighting the fire on the fore-bridge.

Just after one o'clock it was reported to the Captain that the fore-top itself was on fire. The enemy's fire now increased, and the *Inflexible's* guns were ordered to take up rapid fire so as to endeavour to keep it down.*

As soon as the fire on the fore-bridge had been got under sufficiently, Commander Wigram very gallantly went up to the fore-control, burning both his hands severely on the hot iron ladder in doing so, and on reaching the top found Verner standing up, leaning against the side of the control and looking out. He writes: "His injuries were in both fore-arms. He was talking quite sensibly and was very plucky indeed. Blaker had his left leg broken and was hit in one arm but was very plucky and able to talk too. The anxious part was that some matting they had up there to sit on was smouldering, but thank God! it didn't catch alight."

Two of the four wounded seamen were very badly hit and these as well as the two wounded officers were eventually lowered down in ambulance cots, a matter of great difficulty and some danger. Two of the party engaged in clearing the top were wounded.

First-aid was given to the wounded on the bridge below and they were then carried down to the deck below the sick-bay and laid down behind the armour.

At 1.15 both the fore-top and fore-bridge were still on fire and at 1.25 the *Inflexible* left the line and dropped back a mile to extinguish the fires and clear the top of the wounded officers and men. The fires were got under by 2.15 and she at once returned to her position in action and at 2.36 re-opened fire from her heavy guns and soon was as heavily engaged as ever.

About an hour later, at about 3.45 p.m., the Fleet-Surgeon who was attending to the wounded in the Engineers' workshop, where they had been placed below, states that

---

*The photograph on which the picture of the "*Inflexible* in the Attack on the Narrows" was based was taken at this time, about 1.15 p.m., Local Mean Time (G.M.T. 11.15 a.m.), from the Destroyer *Wear*, and shows the general shape of the clouds of smoke about the ship.—ED.

there was a most violent concussion outside the ship within a few feet of Verner's head. Whether this was caused by a heavy projectile striking the armour or by one bursting close to it is uncertain, anyway it did not penetrate but the tremendous shock threw him against the ship's side and further injured his head and caused the wounds of both the officers to start bleeding again and it was necessary to repeat the process of binding them up.

While he lay below Verner neither lost consciousness nor self-control; he asked calmly what was going on above and spoke quietly and cheerfully. Captain Phillimore writes "My steward who was one of the First-Aid Party told me that he was very plucky and was making jokes about his paint-work, etc. His guns, so carefully and successfully trained, were shooting as well on the 18th as they did at the Falkland Islands. I couldn't help thinking that, as he lay wounded, he must have felt some pleasure listening to their rapid fire."*

A little after 4 p.m. the ship struck a mine; this put out the electric lights and naturally caused great discomfort and anxiety to the wounded lying below. The ship was now in a very critical state and in consequence the order was given, "Clear lower deck," and all the wounded were hurriedly carried up, a most unfortunate necessity, since some of them were in a condition that made any movement most hurtful to them.

How critical was the condition of the *Inflexible* at this time can be gathered from the fact that the force of the explosion of the mine had flooded several of the compartments below, and that before long there were some 2,000 tons of water in her.

The *Inflexible* now quitted the line and proceeded slowly out of the Straits. At 5 p.m. three shells passed just fifty yards over her. These were the last fired at her; she had been in action since 11 a.m.

During the course of the action all the boats except one had been rendered unserviceable. This boat was now prepared and slung on the davits and the wounded placed in it,

---

* It is some satisfaction to be able to place upon record the views of the enemy on the good shooting of the British ships in the attack on the Dardanelles of February—March 1915 and more especially the effects of the fire of the *Inflexible* on 18 March. Many months after the Battle of the Narrows the Editor received a letter from Egypt telling him that there among the prisoners was Garfer Pasha of the Turkish Army, who had been Chief of the Staff at the Dardanelles and was subsequently taken prisoner in Egypt. He told the Military Officer in charge of him that the Turks always suffered most during the attack on the Dardanelles in February—March 1915 when the *Inflexible* and the *Irresistible* were firing. How good the *Inflexible* shooting was on the 18 March is testified by Captain (now Vice-Admiral) Sir R. Phillimore, who wrote to the Editor that "Subsequent examination has shown that *Inflexible* knocked out *both* of the 14-inch guns on the Hamidieh Battery (on the European side of the Straits) which was her objective on 18 March."—ED.

FORE CONTROL TOP OF *INFLEXIBLE* AFTER THE ACTION, 18 MARCH, 1915.
From a photograph taken from the forecastle.
(The arrow indicates the point where the fatal shell struck and burst.)

LOWERING THE WOUNDED FROM THE FORE CONTROL TOP OF *INFLEXIBLE*, 18 MARCH, 1915.
(The upper figure is that of Commander Verner.)

Death of Commander Verner

ready for instant lowering, should the ship founder. Whilst the boat was being prepared, the wounded were laid on deck. In spite of the extreme gravity of his wounds Verner still remained conscious and cheery. Several of his brother officers whom he spoke to at this time bear testimony to his extraordinary calmness and fortitude. To one he said "You see I was right about our having a hot time of it. That's the worst of being generally right." Another wrote: "He was most brave about it all; and just before leaving us to be taken to the Hospital Ship *Soudan* he was smoking a cigarette with the aid of a Sub Lieutenant (for both his arms were bandaged) and he had a smile and a word for everyone."

It took about an hour for the *Inflexible* to steam to Tenedos where she anchored at about 6 o'clock. The cutter was sent off at once with the wounded to the Hospital Ship *Soudan* and they were placed on board of her at 6.30 p.m.

The casualties during the day amounted to three officers and thirty men killed or died of wounds, and thirteen men wounded. When, after the Action, the Red Ensign, which had floated so gallantly at the mast-head above the fore-control throughout the day, was hauled down, it was found to have been riddled by the enemy's shrapnel.*

Verner had now done all he could for his Country; he had given his life for the Royal Navy; he was free to think of his parents and his home. His only trouble was the distress he knew his death must cause to his people. He spoke of this to those around him. It was indeed characteristic that his last regret should be that any pain should be caused to those he loved absorbingly and unceasingly. As in his life, so in his death his parents were always in his mind.

"Tell my people," he said to Mr. J. Keogh Murphy who took off his shattered arm, "that I played the game and stuck it out." "Be sure, Sir," said the Surgeon to Verner's father, "he *did* stick it out." Verner's last message was "Tell them I am all right."

He died at 9.38 o'clock on the night of the Battle, 18 March 1915.

At 1.30 p.m. on 19 March the Funeral Party under the charge of Lieutenant Edward Denison left the ship in the Picket-boat. The Ship's Company of the *Inflexible* were all lined up on the quarter- and after-decks and the Band played the "Dead March." The bodies of three Seamen, who had been killed the previous day in the fore-control as well as that of a fourth, were first taken to H.M. Destroyer *Kennet* which was at

19 March (Friday)

---

* This Ensign is now preserved at the Royal Naval School, Greenwich.—ED.

anchor about a mile distant.* The Picket-boat went alongside and transferred the bodies to her, also the Firing Party and the Mourners. The latter consisted of about six Officers and some thirty men. Owing to the very precarious condition of the ship and the amount of work to be done, it was impossible for more to attend.

The *Kennet* weighed anchor at once and went alongside the Hospital Ship *Soudan* and the bodies of Commander Verner and Lieutenant Blaker and those of two more Seamen were transferred on board. All the bodies were sewn up in canvas and weighted.

The *Kennet* then proceeded to sea, passing the *Inflexible* on her way out, the decks of which were still manned, her flag flying at half-mast.

It was blowing hard from the south-west and there was some sea. When about five miles outside, the *Kennet* turned head-to-wind. The Chaplain (the Revd. E. S. Phillips, R.N.) then read the Burial Service and the bodies were committed to the deep, one by one, Commander Verner's first, Lieutenant Blaker's next and then those of the six Seamen. The depth of the water at this spot was thirty fathoms.

As soon as the last body had disappeared beneath the waves the Firing Party of Bluejackets fired three volleys in the air and the Bugler sounded the "Last Post"; then the *Kennet* returned to Tenedos.

"*Si qua fata aspera rumpas*" seems the natural epilogue to such a life. But Rudolf Verner did too much for that. He saw what many a British sailor has longed to see and has not seen, and certainly his end—snatched away in the élan and glory of action—was as he himself would have wished it to be. Yet it is impossible not to dwell on what might have been and what he might have done, had he lived longer. But it was not so ordered.

---

* The bodies of the third officer (the Carpenter) and of the men killed by the mine explosion were recovered later, as the flooded compartments were pumped out.

Memorial Lines

EPILOGUE

In Memoriam

Commander Rudolf H. C. Verner, Royal Navy
Born 16 Jan 1883   Died 18 March 1915
Buried at Sea, off Tenedos

Pro Christo et Patria.
(Motto of the Verners.)

ONCE more from Tenedos comes a tale of heroes!
Fierce roar'd the battle, the battle of the Narrows,
British and French fought for Christ against the Germans,
Preachers of world-might, in force and fraud believers
They, who lay lurking behind their dupes of Turkey.
Then came the warships, " Elizabeth " the greatest,
Towering, strong Queen, with wrath and power flashing;
Near her the undaunted " Inflexible " came floating
Proudly and bravely: a gallant young Commander
Stood in the forefront, the " fore control," directing
Guns that played havoc with strongest Forts and Foemen.
But ere with her crown Victory could adorn him,
Death came and kissed him, and crowned him as a martyr,
With his beloved men who died contented round him,
To Christ and Freedom. The golden bowl was broken:
And o'er his blue grave in ancient Great Sea waters
Greek women scatter'd sweet incense and sweet flowers.

IDA VERNER.

26 *March* 1915.

MEMORIAL WINDOW PLACED IN THE ENGLISH CHURCH
AT ALGECIRAS, SPAIN.

APPENDIX I.

LAST HOURS.

The following documents and letters give further details of Commander Verner's last hours.

MEDICAL REPORT ON COMMANDER VERNER'S WOUNDS.

"Commander Verner was suffering from profound shock and was almost pulseless. The right arm was pulped and most of the hand blown away, requiring removal below the elbow, there was also a large scalp wound with depressed fracture of skull and many wounds of left arm and leg, caused by fragments of shell. His condition made further operation impossible and he died at 9.38 p.m." (From *Journal R.N. Med. Service*, July 1915.)

The following account was given to Mrs. Verner-Jeffreys (Commander Verner's sister) by Nursing Sister Johnston who was with him in the Hospital Ship from the time he came on board until his death.

"He was put into a cot in the men's ward just underneath the operating theatre so as to avoid moving him more than was necessary. He was operated on under chloroform—the doctors and nurse thought he would not survive, but he did and was taken back to the ward and Sister Johnston was with him to the end.

He was conscious at intervals and knew his arm had been amputated for he looked down at his bandaged shoulder when he came to after the operation and said 'I see my arm has gone. Shall I get through this?' He behaved with great pluck and courage all through and gradually passed away, through heart failure. His one message to his father and mother was 'Tell them that I'm all right.'"

Mr. J. Keogh Murphy who operated on Commander Verner in the *Soudan* wrote to the Editor on 9 June 1915,

"He had behaved during the day with great fortitude though he must have well known what his wounds were; he was barely conscious when he came on board and merely asked about me and my capabilities for operating on him. I thought I heard him say before the operation to give his love to his people and tell them he had stuck it out—be this as it may, be sure, Sir, that he *did* stick it out and no one better."

A short time afterwards Mr. Keogh Murphy came to see the Editor and said that he had known Verner well and that only a few days before the Battle had told him a good Irish story which he did not know. Mr. Murphy was an Irishman and an Orangeman and hence there was a bond of union between them, and he described how Verner, in spite of his desperate condition, could not resist the chance, when he saw him in the Hospital Ship, of chaffing him and said "There's that d—d Irishman," and proceeded to ask if he "*felt competent* to operate" on him? Later, Mr. Murphy heard him asking after

Appendix I

" young Blaker." He said that he had removed the shattered arm *above* the elbow, *not below*, as reported. (This fact was corroborated by the Nursing Sister.) He heard him say "Tell my people I played the game and stuck it out."*

From Fleet-Surgeon G. TREVOR COLLINGWOOD, M.V.O., R.N.
(Now Surgeon Rear-Admiral G. TREVOR COLLINGWOOD, C.B., M.V.O.)

Forton Barracks,
Gosport, Hants.
18 Sept. 1915.

DEAR COLONEL VERNER,— . . . . I saw a good deal of your dear son in his last few hours and well remember looking over the ship's side† and seeing him and Blaker with their white and anxious faces lying in the boat. After seeing them hoisted in I went along to one of the Officers' wards and as soon as Verner saw me he gave a little smile and said "Good old Trevor" and later, when I was standing just behind him, said "Is the P.M.O. there?" So I stepped forward to where he could see me and he said "Give me your hand"; so I took his left hand in mine and gently pressed it and again he said "Good old Trevor" and appeared quite happy and resigned. . . . I was with your good son again in the operating room and he said faintly "Is that the P.M.O. there?" So I said "Yes! yes! I'm near by, Verner, old fellow" and he said, "If that is so, I don't mind what is done." So I gently laid my hand on him. Later in the evening he quietly passed away. I was with him at the time and present at the little service read by the Chaplain. . . . As you are well aware, we were formerly shipmates in the *Inflexible* and great friends.

From Captain R. F. PHILLIMORE, R.N., Captain of H.M.S. "Inflexible."
(Now Vice-Admiral Sir RICHARD F. PHILLIMORE, K.C.B., K.C.M.G.)

H.M.S. *Inflexible.*
20 March, 1915.

MY DEAR COLONEL VERNER,—You will already have received the sad news from the Admiralty that your gallant son died of his wounds on the 18th and was buried at sea on the 19th.

We went into action at 11 a.m. against the forts at Chanak but were fired upon by concealed guns and howitzers from both sides of the Dardanelles. At 12.30 a shell struck the fore-top killing three men and wounding the two officers and all the men except one young A.B. up there. Your son was "controlling" the fire at the time and had both arms up looking through his glasses (I enclose the Fleet Surgeon's account of his injuries). He, Lieutenant Blaker and the other wounded were eventually brought down with great difficulty by Wigram, the cabins on the bridge at the foot of the mast being on fire.

---

* It is sad to relate that Mr. J. Keogh Murphy who had a fine reputation as a surgeon and did such excellent work in the Naval Hospitals died after a very short illness at the Royal Naval Hospital, Stonehouse, in the month of September 1915.

† Naval Hospital Ship *Soudan.*

Last Hours

He was placed below armour with the other wounded, but shortly afterwards the ship was heavily hit in the neighbourhood of the Doctor's station, when he began bleeding again.

My Steward who is one of the First Aid Party told me that he was very plucky and was making jokes about his paint-work, etc.

Directly we got to Tenedos, a boat from *Blenheim* took all the wounded on board the Hospital Ship *Soudan* where a Harley Street surgeon with a great reputation took charge of him.

He died that night and Blaker next morning.

The Service has suffered a great loss and one had hoped that his career would have been a very brilliant one.

His guns, so carefully and successfully trained, were shooting as well on the 18th as they did at the Falkland Islands. I couldn't help thinking that, as he lay wounded, he must have felt some pleasure listening to their rapid fire.

Some of his Service papers I am sending to you. His friend, the Gunnery Officer of the *Gneisenau*, will, I know, regret his loss very deeply. Please express my very deep sympathy with Mrs. Verner in her great sorrow and

Believe me,
Yours very sincerely,
RICHARD F. PHILLIMORE.

From Major J. B. FINLAISON, R.M.L.I., H.M.S. "Inflexible."
(Now Colonel J. B. FINLAISON, C.M.G., R.M.L.I.)

H.M.S. *Inflexible*,
Mediterranean Fleet.
Friday 19 March 1915.

DEAR MRS. JEFFREYS,*— . . . . Your letter telling him of your other terrible loss was found in his pocket and I destroyed it. Forgive me, a stranger to you, but not to your father and mother, for writing to say how much we shall miss your brother.

He was such a brilliant and such a clear thinker and hard worker. The Navy will reap benefits from his example and invention for many years to come. He was so proud of his ship and all she had done and was going to do. We shall try and prove his faith in her.

He was most brave about it all and just before leaving us to be taken to H.M. Hospital Ship *Soudan*, he was smoking a cigarette with the aid of a Sub-lieutenant (for both his arms were bandaged) and he had a smile and a word for everyone. . . .

Yours very truly,
J. B. FINLAISON.

H.M.S. *Hussar*.
20 May 1915.

DEAR MRS. VERNER,—Only on the night of the 17th he was talking to me of the hot time we were expecting and he told me he should go up into the fore-control position in addition to Blaker as there would be so much difficulty in directing the fire on the various hostile batteries, which would be on three sides of us. He quite realized that one shell might take two valuable directors of fire at once but would not be

---

* Verner's sister, whose husband, Commander Robert Jeffreys, R.N., Captain of H.M.S. *Clan Macnaughten*, 10th Cruiser Squadron, had been lost at sea, with all his officers and men, some weeks earlier (2-3 February 1915) when on patrol duty in the North Atlantic.

persuaded to try a less exposed position as he said he would not be able to see so well; another proof of his devotion to his Country if such could be needed.

You know of course by this time of the splendid example he set us all of courage under heroic conditions, how he tried to do his duty to the last, how all his thoughts were for the Service, his ship and his comrades. I fortunately had the opportunity to see him and speak to him before he was taken to the *Soudan*, he was talking quite cheerfully then and said "You see I was right about our having a hot time. That's the worst of being generally right." He was able to smile and did not look so very bad.

Yours very sincerely,
J. B. FINLAISON.

Royal Naval Barracks, Plymouth.
19 August 1915.

DEAR COLONEL VERNER,— . . . I did not leave my turret until the ship came out of action.

Without being able to quote exactly what few words I exchanged with your son after he was brought up from below for removal from the ship I still have the impression that he knew he was done for, and yet was cheerful and proud of the part he had been able to take in the action of the day, both from his own point of view and as representative of his own people. He was certainly able to talk when I saw him, indeed I left him because I thought he was taxing his remaining strength by talking too much. He also was smoking with assistance after I had distinctly heard him ask to be given a cigarette. . . .

Yours very sincerely,
J. B. FINLAISON.

From Commander ERNEST WIGRAM, R.N., H.M.S. "Inflexible."
(Now Captain E. WIGRAM, D.S.O., R.N.)

H.M.S. *Inflexible*.
26 April 1915.

DEAR COLONEL VERNER,— . . . . I will try and give you a few details of that unfortunate day. A shell struck the yard just above the control-top and burst, many splinters from the shell coming down through the roof. Rudolf, young Blaker and eight men were up there. Three of the men were killed outright and some of the others managed to get down, assisting each other. This I gather from his orders. One of these, who was only slightly wounded, went up again and was sent down with a message. Rudolf's injuries were in both fore-arms. When I first got up to the top Rudolf was standing up looking out. He was talking quite sensibly and was very plucky indeed. Blaker had his left leg broken and was hit in one arm, but was very plucky and able to talk too. The anxious part was some matting they had up there to sit on was smouldering, but thank God it didn't catch alight. We got them down below to the sick station where they were safe in the doctor's care. Whilst getting him below we had dropped back a mile from the line but then went up again into the line. After we got back we got one or two knocks and then struck a mine which caused a big explosion. These appear to have done all the harm and both Rudolf and Blaker suffered greatly from shock. After the mine explosion all wounded were got up on deck and then into the cutter, our only boat, as no one knew if the ship would stick it or not. I had a short talk with Rudolf before he was put into the cutter and he was really so plucky and cheery. It took us an hour to get back to Tenedos where we anchored. The Fleet Surgeon was with Rudolf in the cutter all the way out. On anchoring they went to the Hospital

Ship and it was a great shock when I heard in the middle watch he had passed away. Blaker died the next morning. I do so sympathize with you and Mrs. Verner in your great loss following immediately after the other. Your son is the greatest loss the ship could have had and not only the ship but the Service, as we know he would have gone to the top.

Yours very sincerely,
ERNEST WIGRAM.

From ALFRED RISEBOROUGH, A.B., Royal Navy, H.M.S. "Inflexible."

R.N. Hospital,
Stonehouse.
7 May 1915.

DEAR MADAM,—About your brother Commander Verner, I only wish I could have rendered better aid but being wounded myself it was impossible.

I cannot speak too highly of him, he was all one could wish for, being liked from the lower deck to the ward room . . . .

If every man did the same what a glorious country it would be!

I am Madam,
Yours truly,
ALF. RISEBOROUGH, A.B.

P.S.—The Ship's Company thought a lot of him for it was through him we won the Cups for Good Shooting.

To Mrs. ROBERT JEFFREYS.

In consequence of this letter the Editor wrote to Alfred Riseborough and received the following letter.

Lilac Farm,
Banningham,
Aylsham.
4 August, 1915.

DEAR SIR,—As far as I can remember we were hit about half past eleven. I could not say for certain how long we lay in the Fore Control after we were wounded but I should think it was not more than one hour. Of course about a quarter of an hour before we were hit the centre tripod was shot through level with Monkey's Island and it caught fire. While that was on fire we got hit and we had to wait for a second fire party to come and put the fire out. While the first party was coming through the stokers' mess-deck, one man was killed and about four wounded. When we recovered from the shock we moved your son on some mats and made him as comfortable as possible. I remember his saying "Thank you, old chap"; he also told us to report us out of action and to ask the Captain to go astern which I am not sure whether it was done. As soon as it was possible A.B. Robinson assisted me down from aloft but Commander Verner, being in a much worse condition than me, I think he was put in bamboo stretcher, but I am not quite sure.

To COLONEL VERNER.   I remain yours truly,
A. R. RISEBOROUGH.

Appendix I

From ARTHUR ROBINSON, A.B., Royal Navy, H.M.S. "Inflexible."

H.M.S. *Inflexible.*
20/4/15.

DEAR SIR,—I am very pleased indeed to oblige you by writing these few lines having been very fortunate to have got out of our Control Top during the action of the 18th March, 1915, being unhurt where your late son, Commander Verner, was severely wounded together with nearly all others in the Control Top. We knew all through that we were in a very exposed place and round after round of shell were fired at us. It was fully two hours before the Fatal Shell struck the Control Top and the Control was put out of action by it, but nevertheless your son still gave his orders, and when brought down to the sick berth, was always asking of the others in the Control Top with him, and how we were getting on during the remainder of the action. Really to have seen him smoking and speaking just as he always was, one would not have thought that it was a serious wound he had got as he made quite light of them. Everyone thought he would have been back with us in a month or so. But he died, which everyone was so sorry to hear, at 9.55 p.m. that night, on the Hospital Ship. I am quite sure that you have everyones' sympathy on this ship, and I do wish I could explain better than by these few lines, but I feel unequal to it, as I am rather a poor hand at writing letters. However if these few lines can convey to you how pluckily he died, I am very proud to pen them. I was very fortunate myself to be unhurt and being one of the last to be with your son, I do sincerely hope that you have an idea by my humble attempt to do so.

I remain yours sincerely,

ARTHUR ROBINSON.

From Lieutenant the Hon. PATRICK ACHESON, R.N., H.M.S. "Inflexible."
(Now Commander Hon. P. ACHESON, D.S.O., R.N.)

H.M.S. *Inflexible*, Gibraltar.
26 April 1915.

DEAR COLONEL VERNER,—It was dreadfully sad losing poor Verner and Blaker and you don't know how much we miss your son both as a messmate and professionally; as the former he was always cheery and kept us in good spirits, as the latter it doesn't want me to eulogize him; you know as well as all of us do how clever both in theory and in practice he was and what an interest he took in the Service. We all feel and deeply sympathize with you in your great loss, a very sad blow and more so as you had only lost your son-in-law a short time before. A heavy price to pay.

I am afraid I can tell you very little as to what occurred on that day, as owing to being in a turret during the action and below on duty whilst making harbour never got a chance of seeing him or saying a word of cheer. The wounded were sent straight away to Hospital Ship almost before the anchor was down. The only time I saw him was during the few minutes when assisting to lower him down from the fore control and then had to return at once to my action station.

A projectile hit the signal yard which is just above the top and burst, pieces all going down through the roof of the control; three of the men were dead, when the first (Commander Wigram) arrived up there, your poor son, Blaker and two men seriously wounded and one slightly; it was about 12.30.

Your son still gave his orders as long as he could, then informed Captain being unable to carry on any longer. He was given First Aid on the bridge and then taken down to hospital. He kept on asking how the action was going and what damage we were doing to the enemy, also after his wounded shipmates. Just before getting to the boat to go to the Hospital Ship he was smoking and smiling as if nothing was the matter and talking when all the time he must have known. I think before we went into action he had the feeling that it was to be his last. We had a cocktail together just after "Action" had been sounded and remember that passing my mind, why I don't know. . . . Dear Colonel Verner I cannot tell you how much I feel for you and Mrs. Verner. The Nation can never thank men like you who have given *everything* to her in her need.

Anyway I feel certain that Rudolf is happy in having died fighting bravely for his Country.

Yours sincerely,
PATRICK ACHESON.

From Fleet-Paymaster HENRY HORNIMAN, R.N., H.M.S. "Inflexible."
(Now Paymaster-Commander H. HORNIMAN, R.N.)

H.M.S. *Inflexible.*
15 October 1915.

DEAR COLONEL VERNER,—Your son's injuries were much more extensive than we imagined at the time. . . . While Meaden (the Fleet-Surgeon) was engaged with him I was with Martin (Surgeon) looking after Blaker, the seaman, Riseborough, who was also brought down from the fore-top, having been more easily (on account of the nature of his wounds) made more comfortable first. It was while looking after Blaker that I had two or three messages from your son, who, on my going over to him, then asked me how "the boy" (Blaker) was getting on. I had some general conversation with him about the whole affair, and he was very cheerful and lucid.

The three were, from the fore-top, brought to a position behind armour (not the regular Sick Bay, which is on the unarmoured deck above) in the Engineers' workshop. This compartment runs across the ship, on the deck below that with the port-holes, just before the after-turret. Your son was laid athwart-ship on the starboard side with his head about four feet from the armoured hull. Blaker was fore-and-aft with his head a couple of yards from the other's feet.

After they had been down some time and when we had done all that was then possible for Blaker, but whilst Meaden was still engaged with your son, a projectile (a considerable one from the shock and clatter, but not large enough to penetrate the 6-inch armour) burst, as I should judge it, on the hull within a few feet of your son's head. It was this projectile, I believe, which started both the wounded officers bleeding again and a readjustment of bandages, etc., was necessary. Myself, I think that had your son's head been left by the first wounding so slightly hurt that he was able to retain his senses, the violence of this shock was sufficient to very materially increase the damage.

It was a while after this that the mine exploded and I did not speak to him in the interval. The explosion took place forward, on the same side, under water (20 feet, say) at the position of the fore-turret. The effect was to heave and shake the whole ship, to put all the electric light out, but there was no violence of shock where we were aft.

Some five or ten minutes after this the order to " clear lower deck" was given and as the imminence of danger to the ship was not known below, it was necessary to get the wounded on deck as expeditiously as possible. I don't think that this handling could have been helpful (although as gentle as possible) and subsequently there was a period on deck when we were coming out under the shrapnel fire of the enemy; a period in the boat at the davits going across to Tenedos and standing by in case of the ship's foundering; the transference to the Hospital Ship. All cumulative in its effect. The series of shocks, plus the lack of rest and quiet, must have been most maleficent. . . .

Yours very truly,
HENRY HORNIMAN.

Appendix I

From the Revd. ERNEST S. PHILLIPS, M.A., R.N.

H.M.S. *Inflexible*,
Mediterranean Fleet.
22 March 1915.

DEAR COLONEL VERNER,—Please allow me to offer you my deepest sympathy at the sad loss of your son.

His was a very gallant and noble end and I understand that his last thought was for others.

Two years constant association with him has only tended to confirm my opinion of him, not only as a very fine officer but as a courteous Christian gentleman, ever ready with his sympathy and anxious at all times to give his help to those who needed it. His loss is very much felt in our Mess and his place will be a hard one to fill.

Believe me,
Yours very truly,
ERNEST S. PHILLIPS, Chaplain.

The following is an extract from a letter from Major Finlaison to an intimate friend of Verner's in England.

H.M.S. *Inflexible*.
15 April 1915.

"The ship was in action for some six hours on the 18th of March and for most of that time she was under fairly heavy fire. Most unfortunately a shell burst quite close to our fore-top where our brilliant gunnery man was directing our fire, practically without the slightest protection. If it can be any comfort it is true that he was so badly hit as to be without serious pain, though he kept a clear brain, which only thought of victory and others till he was taken to the *Soudan* Hospital Ship.

I am glad to feel that I had a few words with him after the action was over. He had told me the night before that he expected we should have all the fighting we wanted and reminded me of this as he lay waiting on the upper deck until he could be taken away to more comfortable surroundings.

He had a smile and a word and a thought for everyone but himself although both his arms were useless and his head struck as well.

Commander Wigram, who went up to the top to get them down, told me he found Verner leaning over the edge of the control position trying to give orders though he was practically knocked out. I am sure he was too far gone to have suffered much pain and he certainly was not doing so when I saw him, for he said so to me; only he was afraid his people would be distressed to hear about it all, for he knew he was dying.

We have lost a hero, but it will do us all good to remember his splendid character and try to live somewhere nearly up to it. You will be glad to know that just because of his system of training and trust that everyone would do their best in his absence, the ship was able to do some good shooting afterwards and to help in subsequent events of a fine fighting day.

We have lost a good officer and splendid comrade and we are all rather sad, but when things are put right we shall be there again with an example before us which will never be forgotten.

We buried him at sea about three miles south of the Island of Tenedos where he lies close to his friend Blaker."

APPENDIX II.

LETTERS.

From H.M. THE KING.

(By Rear-Admiral Sir Colin Keppel, K.C.I.E., K.C.V.O., C.B., D.S.O., Equerry to H.M.)

Buckingham Palace,
22 March 1915.

DEAR VERNER,—Only a few days ago I wrote to Harry Stephenson by the King's desire asking him to convey to you the King's sympathy with you in the great loss of your son-in-law and his congratulations on your son's promotion.

I now write again by His Majesty's command to express to you his sympathy with you in the loss of your gallant son who he has just heard has died from wounds received in the engagement off the Dardanelles. The King feels it will be some small consolation to you when you think that your son died doing his duty to his Country.

As an old comrade up the Nile may I add my own personal sympathy with you in your great grief.

Believe me,
Yours sincerely,
COLIN KEPPEL.

From H.M. THE QUEEN OF SPAIN.

Telegrama.

Madrid,
le 31 de Marzo 1915.

Al Coronel Verner, Algeciras.

S. M. La Reina Victoria me encargo le dijese su sentimiento por perdidas sufridas.

CONDÉ DEL RINCON.

From Admiral Sir ARCHIBALD BERKELEY MILNE, Bt., G.C.V.O., K.C.B.

3 Down Street, Piccadilly, W.
25 March 1915.

MY DEAR COLONEL,—Allow me to express to both Mrs. Verner and yourself the most profound sympathy which I feel for you in the great loss you have sustained. Your son's loss is a loss to the Navy. As you are aware, I have known him for many years. I had a great admiration for him, clever, quick, and most zealous in the performance of his duties.

Yours very sincerely,
A. BERKELEY MILNE.

Appendix II

From Commodore ROGER KEYES, Chief of the Staff to the Vice-Admiral Commanding Eastern Mediterranean Squadron.

(Now Vice-Admiral Sir ROGER KEYES, Bart., K.C.B., K.C.V.O., C.M.G., D.S.O.)

H.M.S. *Queen Elizabeth*,
11 May 1915.

MY DEAR MRS. VERNER,—I have been meaning to write to you for a long time about your gallant "Dodo's" death. I know Captain Phillimore has written all there is to say about it to Colonel Verner, but I thought you would like to hear from such an old friend which I hope I may call myself. I was in the *Inflexible* for about a month but left her shortly before the action of 18th March so anything I can say is only second hand, but I have heard how gallantly "Dodo" met his fate and with what fortitude he bore his wounds, chaffing those attending him—his chief concern being the condition of his companion in the top—Blaker. In fact he died very gallantly—an example to those about him. It was a cruel fate, for he had done so well and had such a very promising future.

I was so distressed to hear of Robert Jeffreys' death and I do sympathize most deeply with Dorothy. "Dodo" and I were talking about it only a few days before his death. There is so little one can say at these times but I do sympathize with you three in your great sorrow and I wanted to tell you so.

Yours very sincerely,
ROGER KEYES.

In the Falkland Action the Gunnery Officer who directed so well the fire of the Flagship (H.M.S. *Invincible*) was Lieutenant-Commander H. E. Dannreuther. For his services on that day he was promoted Commander and was re-appointed to the *Invincible* for Gunnery duties. Among the first letters the Editor received after the death of his son was the following:—

From Commander H. E. DANNREUTHER, R.N., Gunnery Officer, H.M.S "Invincible,"

(Now Captain H. E. DANNREUTHER, D.S.O., R.N.)

H.M.S. *Invincible*,
25 March 1915.

DEAR COLONEL VERNER,—May I be allowed to express my deep sorrow for the irreparable loss of your son. We all feel his loss very much in this ship—a brave man and a gallant gentleman.

Yours sincerely,
H. E. DANNREUTHER.

In a subsequent letter Commander Dannreuther wrote to the Editor to say how "Everyone who was at the Falklands knows how splendidly the *Inflexible* did on that day"

Letters

From Brigadier-General The EARL OF LUCAN (formerly Rifle Brigade).

Malta.
26 March 1915.

MY DEAR VERNER,—I have only just heard the sad news by the Hospital Ship *Soudan* which has come in here with wounded from the Dardanelles. And I must write a line to let you and Mrs. Verner know how much we are thinking of you at this sad time. I was only talking to him in the Club here on Sunday week when the *Inflexible* had come back for two days to change her guns—and he was so nice and cheery, and I thought so sound in his estimate of the situation and its difficulties, and everybody seemed devoted to him, and Collingwood, one of the senior surgeons on the *Soudan* who had served with him in the *Inflexible*, is quite miserable. Of course no human sympathy is much consolation in a loss like yours, but I thought I must send a line to tell you how sorry we are for you both.

Yours ever,
BINGHAM.

From Commander EDWARD A. RUSHTON, R.N., Shipmate with Verner in H.M.S. "Albemarle."
(Now Captain E. ASTLEY-RUSHTON, C.M.G., R.N.)

H.M.S. *Southampton*,
22.3.15.

DEAR COLONEL VERNER,—I write not only to offer my deepest sympathy for I know that can help you but little but also to tell you how sincerely and deeply one of your son's old friends shares your grief. You, Sir, have lost an only son and I have lost a very dear, and I had hoped, life-long friend and my wife feels it almost as much as I do. We, his friends, who knew him intimately and were privileged to see beneath the mask he chose to wear, were able to assay the gold of his character and to plumb the depths of his strong feelings—feelings unguessed by the crowd who saw the débonair merry exterior—and we loved him. I remember, Sir, not very long ago when he was full of anxiety on account of you, his father and comrade, how his great moral courage enabled him to leave the majority of his shipmates entirely unaware that anything was wrong in his world and I thought of the old tag "The man worth while is the man who can smile, when everything goes dead wrong" which fitted him exactly. The Navy has lost a gallant and brilliant officer. We, his friends, can never lose him entirely, for his memory will be ever green and cared for. But for us the world can never again be the same; a great gap is torn which cannot be filled.

Believe me,
Yours most sincerely,
E. A. RUSHTON.

From Kapitain-Leutnant HANS BUSCH, late of S.M.S. "Gneisenau." (A Prisoner of War.)

Holyport.
10 August, 1915.

DEAR SIR,—Your kind letter of July 22 received. I was indeed very much depressed to get by you the confirmation of the death of your son, which I happened to read in the newspaper. Please accept my heartfelt consolation to this hard loss which you and your family are suffering. I assure you I shall always remember your late son as a kind, clever, and gallant officer, whose ability and courtesy I had the opportunity to admire during and after the action off Falkland Islands.

Three days before I read the news in the roll of honour I had a cheerful letter from your son; unfortunately his death put a stop to our correspondence. During my stay on board H.M.S. "Inflexible" we talked often about the details of the battle and I would only be pleased after the conclusion of the war to converse with you about the matter. Again assuring you the admiration I felt for your brave son, the late Commander Verner, R.N., I remain with my sincerest regards,

Yours faithfully,

HANS BUSCH, *Kapitain-leutnant.*
Gunnery-lieutenant of the late S.M.S. *Gneisenau.*
Prisoner of War 192, Holyport.

From J. C. TREGARTHEN, Esq., Master at Verner's First School.

DEAR COLONEL VERNER,—I deeply regret the death of Rudolf. I recall him a bright, brilliant boy full of the promise which he has lived only partly to fulfil. There may be as good men in the Navy, There cannot be better

With sincere sympathy,

I am yours,

J. C. TREGARTHEN.

From Mrs. LAURENCE CURRIE.

Minley Manor,
Farnborough, Hants.
4 April 1915.

MY DEAR COLONEL VERNER,— . . . . His fine good life is not easily written about and those who loved him best feel they could never do him justice. It is that he was a bit *too fine* for the general world to understand and really appreciate, but all *loved* him. About here in the house it was the same "a friend had gone," "one who was always the same," "one who had always a kind word and look" and "one who was *a man* and a very useful one."

These are a few of the things said: and then letters:—"Tell me! it is not true—our Sailor boy?" "God grant it is not our Verner, say it is someone else of that name," etc. . . . But what a glorious death! . . . But his life was such that you can look on it with perfect joy, he was so straight, true, loyal, brave and fine, so loving and tender, so joyous and brilliant, one felt better for seeing him, stronger for a grasp of his hand. And he died as he would fain do, facing the foe at his post. . . .

Yours and his friend,

SIBYL CURRIE.

Minley Manor,
Farnborough, Hants.
22 March, 1915.

MADAM,—On behalf of the Household Staff here, please accept our heartfelt sympathy in your great sorrow. We were all so fond of him, especially those of us who have been fortunate enough to know him since his boyhood days.

In respectful sympathy,

To The HON. MRS. VERNER.   T. E. GWILLIAM, *House Steward.*

Letters

From The Hon. BERNARD ROLLO.

Castle Malwood,
Lyndhurst, Hants.
4 July, 1915.

MY DEAR VERNER,—I have long tried to write you a line but have failed to be able to express all I feel about your great loss. He was so much more than a son, for there was that great love and admiration you had for each other that only exists in the closest friendship and when that comes to an end, to the one left it is as the disappearance of daylight.

I cannot tell you how much I feel for you, for I really loved "Dodo" for his great charm. I admired him for his courage and brilliance of intellect and his kindly heart and his intense sense of humour. I do feel his loss greatly but his magnificent end and the courage in the way he met it is what I knew and expected

Believe me,
Yours very sincerely,
B. ROLLO.

To COLONEL WILLOUGHBY VERNER.

From Lieutenant The Lord CONGLETON, Royal Navy.

H.M.S. *Newcastle.*
25 April, 1915.

DEAR UNCLE WILLOUGHBY,—I am writing to say how awfully sorry I was to see "Dodo's" name in the casualty lists . . . . He will be a tremendous loss to the Service, the more so as he was one of the comparatively few Naval Officers who have had experience in a proper Naval Action.

Yours affectionately,
JACK PARNELL.

To COLONEL WILLOUGHBY VERNER.

From JOHN JEFFREYS, Esq., of Canterton Manor, Lyndhurst.*

. . . . He was one of the most charming companions that I ever met and the Nation has lost a fine type of Naval Officer. He fell doing his duty and in defence of his Country but we can ill afford to lose such men

---

From FRED. T. VERNER, Esq.

. . . . His death is a great loss to us all. He was a splendid fellow with fine abilities and pluck and was making a great name for himself and leaves many friends to mourn his untimely fate.

---

* Father-in-law of Verner's sister.

APPENDIX III.

EXTRACTS FROM OFFICIAL REPORTS AND DESPATCHES RELATING TO THE SERVICES OF COMMANDER RUDOLF H. C. VERNER AT THE ACTION OF THE FALKLAND ISLES AND THE OPERATIONS IN THE DARDANELLES.

(1) THE ACTION OF THE FALKLAND ISLES.

Extracts from Captain of Inflexible's *Report on Falkland Action.*

"It is a matter of peculiar satisfaction that despite the severity of the test, the Gunnery Organization worked well throughout, both as regards personnel and materiel."

* * * *

(Followed a "Mention" of Lieutenant-Commander Verner.)

* * * * *

"I have already referred to the efficiency of the Gunnery arrangements for which the Senior and Gunnery Lieutenant of the ship is responsible.

He is an Officer of unusual ability."

The Lords of the Admiralty have given permission for it to be recorded here that Lieutenant-Commander Rudolf H. C. Verner, Royal Navy, was "mentioned" by Vice-Admiral Sir Frederick Doveton Sturdee in his Despatches on the Action of the Falkland Isles on 8 December 1914.

(2) OPERATIONS IN THE DARDANELLES.

Extracts from Despatch of Vice-Admiral S. H. CARDEN *describing the Attack on the Outer Forts on 19 February 1915, dated 17 March 1915.*
(*Published in a Supplement to the London Gazette of Tuesday, 29 April 1919*)

H.M.S. *Queen Elizabeth.*

"11.45 a.m. *Inflexible* opened on Fort No. 1 . . the practice appeared good.

* * * *

1.0 p.m. *Inflexible* opened fire on Fort No. 3, making good practice.

* * * *

5.0 p.m. *Inflexible* opened fire on Fort No. 4 with the immediate effect of causing her fire to suffer in accuracy."

(3) ACTION OF THE DARDANELLES.

Extract from Captain of Inflexible's *Report of Action of 18 March 1915 in the Dardanelles.*

"I deeply regret to report that Commander Rudolf Henry Cole Verner, Royal Navy (borne in lieu of a Lieutenant (G), and Lieutenant Arthur Wilfred Blaker, Royal Navy, who were in the fore-top controlling, have since died of their wounds on board the Hospital Ship *Soudan*. Both Officers are a great loss to His Majesty's Navy and did very good service in the Action on 8 December 1914."

Extract from Despatch of Vice-Admiral J. M. DE ROBECK.
(*Published in a Supplement to the London Gazette of Tuesday, 29 April 1919*)

Queen Elizabeth,
26 March 1915.

. . . . The ships received little damage by the enemy's gun-fire, although the annoyance from concealed batteries on both sides of the Straits was very great. It was evident that some of these batteries were directing their fire at the control positions of the ships. In this way the *Inflexible* lost two very fine officers who were in her fore control, viz., Commander Rudolf H. C. Verner and Lieutenant Arthur W. Blaker.

APPENDIX IV.

THE SUBSEQUENT WAR-HISTORY OF THE *INFLEXIBLE*.

The sorely-stricken *Inflexible*, which had anchored in shoal water north of Tenedos on the evening of 18 March, owing to a northerly gale springing up about forty-eight hours afterwards, slipped her cables and moved to the south of the island, and later to Mudros Bay in the Island of Lemnos where some temporary repairs were carried out. The great rent in her bottom, which measured no less than twenty feet by thirty feet, was covered by a "pad" and a coffer-dam built inside of it. On 6 April she left for Malta, being "cheered out" by the British and French Ships, escorted by the *Canopus* and *Talbot* and after a hazardous voyage, during which the "pad" worked loose and she was in danger of foundering, she was eventually towed stern-first by the *Canopus* for the last six hours and then "slipped" to windward of the Grand Harbour which she entered under her own steam. The bastions were crowded with people, though it was after dark, and the effect was very impressive. At Malta she was temporarily repaired and then proceeded to Gibraltar where she was docked and all damages made good. As soon as this was effected she went to the North Sea and joined the Grand Fleet under Sir John Jellicoe on 19 June, exactly three months after she had been so badly "knocked out" in the Dardanelles.

At the Battle of Jutland on 31 May 1916 she formed part of the 3rd Battle Cruiser Squadron consisting of the *Invincible*, flying the flag of Rear-Admiral Hon. Horace Hood, the *Indomitable* and some Light Cruisers. The Squadron steaming in line-ahead, *Invincible* leading, followed by the *Inflexible* and *Indomitable*, came into action at about 5.40 p.m. with some of the enemy's light cruisers at about 8,000 yards range. Soon after 6 the enemy's light cruisers launched their torpedoes (one of which passed under the *Inflexible*) and then turned and fled; one of them was badly on fire and later on blew up. Beatty with the 1st Battle Cruiser Squadron was now engaging the enemy. At 6.20 p.m. the 3rd Battle Cruiser Squadron was engaged by the leading enemy ship at about 8,600 yards, as well as with three of the enemy's Battleships, and the *Inflexible* obtained several direct hits on a battleship of the *Kaiser* or *König* class. A furious fight now followed, the enemy's salvos straddling our Cruisers at 8,000 yards. At 6.30 p.m. the gallant Hood hailed Commander Dannreuther (who was in the fore-control station of the *Invincible*) saying that the firing was "very good" and that he was to keep it up as quickly as possible, for every shot was telling. Four minutes later a shell struck the *Invincible* at "Q" turret and she blew up. Of the whole ship's company, about 1,031, only Commander Dannreuther with one other officer and four men were saved.

It is a curious coincidence that of the two Gunnery Officers who, between them, sank the *Scharnhorst* and *Gneisenau*, the exposed situation in the fore control led to the death of the one and assisted in the escape of the other.

Jellicoe stated in his account that the *Invincible* had engaged an enemy battleship and *not* a battle cruiser as was imagined at the time. When the *Invincible* sank, the *Inflexible* became "leader of the line" and it is gratifying to record that her gunnery, as ever, stood her in good stead and, in the words of one who wrote to the Editor about the Action, "the old ship did a power of damage and got more than her own back" as a solace for the heavy handling she had experienced in the Dardanelles.

Thus the good gunnery of the *Inflexible* once again drew praise. Few ships if any of our glorious Navy in the whole course of the Great War saw more fighting than did the *Inflexible*, some say she saw more than any. It is certain that few ships have survived such tremendous damages as she received in the Dardanelles or have fired more heavy shell than she did in her various encounters. During the War she fired no less than 952 of her 12-inch shells at the enemy.

For a sailor like Rudolf Verner, who literally gave his life to the study and advancement of Gunnery in the Royal Navy, it would be hard to find a more suitable "Honour and Reward" than the assurance that the guns and the guns' crews he had trained had justified his work so well.

APPENDIX V.

EXTRACTS FROM "GRAF SPEE'S LAST CRUISE," by Fregatten-kapitäin Hans Pochhammer, Executive Officer of S.M.S. *Gneisenau*.

THE ACTION OFF THE FALKLAND ISLANDS.

[NOTE.—After the Coronel Action on 1 November 1914, the German Cruiser Squadron (*Scharnhorst*, Flagship of Count Spee, *Gneisenau, Nürnberg, Dresden, Leipzig*) proceeded leisurely northwards. The first three vessels put into Valparaiso on 3 November, leaving again the next day and anchoring off Mas-á-Fuera on the morning of 6 November. On 15 November the Squadron left "proceeding southwards towards a new and unknown future." At daybreak on 21 November they anchored in the Gulf of Penas. On the afternoon of 26 November they put to sea again, bound round the Horn, which was sighted "in the distance far away to port" on 2 December. The Beagle Channel was entered that night and the ships anchored at 5 a.m. on 3 December to the east of Picton Island. At noon on 6 December they left, proceeding along the southern coast of Terra del Fuego, and thence past Staten Island *en route* for the Falklands. 7 December was occupied in "preparing for a landing and action."]

The night was bright, just as when we put into Picton Sound, and visibility was extraordinarily good, even at an early hour. From about 2 a.m. on 8 December we could see dark specks on the horizon and soon we were able to recognize land—the Falkland Islands.

At 5 a.m. the *Gneisenau* and the *Nürnberg* parted company from the Squadron to carry out the purposed raid. At increased speed we proceeded northward, the other ships continuing on their old course and gradually becoming smaller until at last there was nothing but their smoke to be seen over the horizon. Our objective, on the other hand, was more clearly visible every hour. It was long past daybreak and the ship swarmed with men going about their various duties. A keen morning air was blowing as the cliffs, bays and hills of the British Coast ahead came into sight and were entered in the log. The sea was calm, only a light north-west breeze fluttering its surface; the sky was a brilliant blue. Suddenly on our starboard bow where Cape Pembroke lighthouse marks the entrance, a thin column of smoke seemed to detach itself from the horizon, drifting quickly to port towards Stanley Harbour. The latter, as well as the extended outer basin of Port William, were invisible from the southward owing to a long chain of hills. As we approached, however, signs of animation became apparent. At intervals clouds of yellowish-black smoke burst out of the dunes, drifted together and spread out again, so that it looked as if stores had been set on fire to prevent them from falling into our hands. We had evidently been observed, for two of the masts which had appeared among the smoke clouds detached themselves and moved slowly to eastward, towards the lighthouse. The *Gneisenau* and *Nürnberg* at once increased speed with a view to catching the outgoing cruiser in the entrance if possible, for there was no longer any doubt that war vessels were there, lying behind the shelter of the smoke and the land. We thought we could make out two, then four, and finally six vessels in succession, and reported them by wireless to the *Scharnhorst*.

According to the terms of our mission, however, Graf Spee had no intention whatever of giving battle here off the Falkland Islands. As our opponents seemed to be inferior to us, partly in speed and partly in fighting value, he was justified in the hope that he could shake them all off before nightfall if they should pursue us. With full confidence in the excellent condition of our boilers and engines and the men who served them, the Admiral therefore gave orders to break off the enterprise and close on the Flagship. Before we had even replied to the few rounds with which we were welcomed from the inner Harbour and which fell into the water alongside, both ships turned to on easterly course and joined the Squadron rather more than an hour later. We then proceeded in company, increasing speed as the boilers permitted, gradually altering course to starboard, with due consideration for our convoy to the southward.

But fate, which had hitherto been so kind to us, had ordained otherwise. The sun blazed down on

Extracts from "Graf Spee's Last Cruise"

us relentlessly, there was neither wind nor cloud, so that visibility in that cold air exceeded anything known to seafaring experience. But we had to make the best of it, and, having once seen the lion ready to spring, were ready to meet him. Nor was it long before his strength began to make itself felt. Two vessels began to detach themselves from amongst our pursuers, apparently larger and faster than the rest, for their smoke was thicker and became more solid. Once again every pair of binoculars was turned on to them to try and make out distinguishing marks on the hulls which were almost enveloped in smoke. Are they Japs? In that case they must have passed us or have come across from the other side of the Atlantic. I did not believe it. The only possibility, in fact probability, was that they were British Battle Cruisers on our track, and our hearts stood still for a moment. For this meant a fight to the death, even though a glorious death. "Don't imagine that it will always be as plain sailing as at Coronel; it may turn out differently next time." A warning I had issued to the ship's company flashed into my mind as we tore along at lightning speed, the white foam splashing on our grey hulls. There was no help for it. The heavens remained clear; not a vestige of a cloud was to be seen to give a promise of bad weather, no friendly mist offered us shelter from the oncoming foe. At roll call late that morning the crew were reminded that a hot fight lay before them, and with determination we anticipated the next few hours.

About midday two Battle Cruisers, converging slightly towards each other, were about 170 hectometres (18,592 yds.) on our port quarter, four other cruisers further astern in line abreast, while the smoke of two more vessels drifted out of the harbour in a southerly direction where we assumed the *Seydlitz*, *Baden* and *Santa Isabella* to be. Dinner was served at the usual hour 11.45 a.m., but it was a quiet meal, everyone being occupied with his own thoughts. Whilst we were still at table a dull rumbling as of distant thunder was plainly audible and drum and bugle soon summoned us to action stations.

I proceeded first to the Captain on the bridge to receive his final orders and inform myself of the position of affairs before descending to my iron dungeon. The foremost enemy ship which was still at 160 hectometres (17,498 yds.) away, had opened fire on the last in our line, the *Leipzig*, with heavy guns, as was evident from the high columns of water rising on either side of her. Some shells were also falling alongside the *Scharnhorst* which was following the *Gneisenau* : the enemy had come within range and was "roaring out his summons to action."

But we had no intention of letting ourselves be quietly shot at, one after another. Every nerve must be strained, even though we appeared to be overborne by superior force. The shot-riddled flag of Coronel waving over our heads demanded it.

There was nothing to be gained by retaining the light cruisers any longer, so with a heavy heart the Commander-in-Chief dismissed them, covering their reluctant retreat by an attack on the enemy's far superior forces with the *Scharnhorst* and *Gneisenau*.

Whilst we were gazing after the *Leipzig*, *Nürnberg* and *Dresden*, which were turning away in a short semi-circle to starboard and disappearing rapidly, to make their escape singly, the *Gneisenau* with her helm hard over was following in the wake of the flagship, which was also turning to port on to a N.E. course. We were just able to see that the more distant enemy ships were proceeding to chase our light cruisers. Then we were left alone with the Battle Cruisers which belonged to the *Invincible* class, and the game of the iron dice could begin. Only one solitary three-masted sailing vessel, passing close by in the rays of the noonday sun with all sail set, was witness to the unequal combat which ensued.

The two lines had hardly settled on their new courses when—it must have been soon after 1 o'clock—the *Scharnhorst's* first broadside swept across the water, striking the British flagship at 154 hectometres (16,842 yds.). Who would have dreamt in days gone by of such a distance, the very utmost range of our guns, which were pointing upwards at their greatest inclination. Everywhere there was the usual scene of calm routine at all stations. The ammunition party thundered dully overhead as they received the shells and cartridges, placed them in trollies and dashed off with them to the guns. The air was filled with the whirr of the electric fans. The indicator on the revolution gauge played round 115; so we were making over 21 knots. Words of command sounded to us from the turret. Order transmitters creaked,

Appendix V

whistles and reports came down the voice pipes, and the floor of the control room heaved and trembled as each salvo droned on its way.

Battle music! The finest of all. It soothed the nerves worn out by the long morning of suspense, turned mere men into iron fighting machines, and at each round fired, each hit received, the crew were more firmly welded together in inveterate determination to give to their utmost. The enemy were still finding the range. The 30.5 cm. shells, which each of his ships was firing from her eight guns, fell to right and left of us, throwing up columns of water like sheaves, reaching to the top of the masts and swamping us when driven over to us by the wind.

Then came the first hit. It grazed the third funnel and burst on the superstructure deck above the after starboard 21 cm. casemate. Large splinters passed through the 15 cm. casemates and the armoured deck, right into the coal bunker. One officer had both arms shattered, a messenger was severely wounded, and several other men slightly; a stoker of the leak-stopping party was seen to fall. The first blood of the battle had been drawn and our first man had been killed. The stretcher parties and doctors went about their work and the dead man was laid in the blacksmith's shop. Others proceeded to repair the damage done to the ship. An iron ring below decks, which served to fix coal shoots, had been loosened and impeded the action of the 21 cm. guns; the foot-board had been bent. The splinters were quickly removed from the cog wheels and the guns reported clear. The funnel, too, was soon patched up so that the draught of the boilers was not inferfered with. A second hit followed, tore open the port side near the middle deck and spread devastation in its wake, but without impairing our fighting efficiency. Then came the report that the after-part had been hit, but only by a long splinter which must have been from a "short" and which had struck the ship close to the water, ripping open the sloping armoured deck and penetrating the magazine below it. There was a smell of fire, so the men were hastily hauled out through the shaft and speedily recovered from unconsciousness, and the magazine was flooded to avert an explosion and consequent danger to the vessel. It contained mostly ammunition for the lighter guns which would not come into action to-day owing to the distance. If only the range had not been so extraordinarily great, we would soon have shown the British what our guns could do. As it was the Commander-in-Chief was able, by lying up to the enemy, to reduce the distance somewhat; 150, 140, 130, 120, even 110 hectometres (12,030 yards) were successively recorded, facilitating observation of the effect of the shells on the target, so that the salvos followed each other more rapidly. The British Admiral must have observed then, from the greater effectiveness of our guns, what we were capable of, and after an action of three-quarters of an hour turned away to the northward! The day was yet young and his victory was assured. The more cheaply and safely he secured it, the better for himself but the worse for us. He was to windward of us. Hence his ships from our position were enveloped in thick smoke and he could only have had a bad view of us. Did he intend to improve his position? Perhaps to lure us into following him and then eluding us by his superior speed? Or did he want to see to his fires, which apparently consumed a lot of oil? Well, anyhow Graf Spee did not follow him, but turned away to southward, the most likely direction where thick weather might be encountered. Every moment saved before nightfall might decide our fate. The engines were still undamaged and were giving of their best, although it was probable that after such a long sojourn in the tropics our ships were no longer capable of their full speed.

The two opponents proceeded away from each other at topmost speed, and in this interval we had time to survey our injuries and report to the Admiral. The damage to the casemates had already been repaired when I arrived there, but the middle deck was a sight to behold. There was a gaping hole in the side. Iron bars, rails and deck-plates had been broken, bent, rolled up, hurled about all over the place. Both the cutters which had been fixed in their crutches were shattered; the pulling boat had her stern blown away. The sea water in the boats had swamped the deck and, pouring through a large hole, had flooded the midshipmen's mess, putting out a fire which had broken out there among the berths and kit. Splinters had flown through the serving-trap hatch into the officers' mess and had made a clean sweep of the tables still laid for lunch. Our little black pigs had also been hit, so a kindly revolver shot ended their sufferings. The goose however had survived and was cackling among the overturned potatoes, while the pigeons were calmly flying about and sitting on the battered nettings, a picture of peace in the midst of war. We quickly removed whatever *débris* was likely to be in the way, for the enemy apparently did not mean to give us much time. He had swung round to take up the chase again and was slowly but steadily gaining upon us. At about 170 hectometres (18,592 yards) the foremost ship again opened fire. But to hit back was beyond the range of possibility. Although the enemy's shells had fallen ahead of the *Scharnhorst* in our line, the Commander-in-Chief quietly waited until the distance was reduced to 150 hectometres (16,404 yards). He then turned to port and resumed the action at about 2.30 p.m. Once more both lines were proceeding abreast at utmost speed. Again with the wind astern, thick smoke from the funnels and guns obscured the target, so that, beside the masts, there was little to be seen beyond the stern. Once more we tried to reduce the distance, but this time the enemy took good care not to let us approach too close; and we realized that our last action had begun, that our pleasant voyaging and cruiser warfare had ended for ever, that the sun was shining for the last time on our proud Cruiser Squadron. But not a man failed for all that. . . . Death was very busy aboard, and it was merely a question of whom he would take first. A shell fell in the galley-deck, shattering the men's galley between the 21 cm. casemates, and at the sides, the gunnery transmitting stations. A loud dull crash resounded with the noise of breaking steel; smoke and steam filled the room and escaped through the huge gap in the deck. The Battery officer, whose narrative I quote here, with his two observers had been thrown to the floor, but had been saved from a worse fate by the hammocks. They picked themselves up and beheld a scene of desolation; the tin walls of the galley had been hurled in all directions, the huge cooking vessels had been smashed, the men—reserves and stretcher-bearers—killed and mutilated, hurled by the air pressure, and crushed, their clothing split at the seams or torn bodily off them. But heavy as the loss was, the guns were still there and could be fired from some other point. Their crews were carrying on as though nothing had happened. In all the casemates the picture was the same; men with blackened faces and arms carrying out their allotted duties amid the stifling fumes of powder; guns creaking as they moved in and out; cheery shouts from the officers, monotonous reports from the order transmitters, and the shrill ringing of the salvo bells. Unrecognizable corpses were laid on one side, and if time permitted covered with a flag; the walls are spattered with blood. But who cared? The action was in full swing, one's whole nervous system adjusted to it, and the shells were now falling more frequently. Owing to the great distance they came over at a steep angle and consequently more often hit the thin armoured decks than the thick side-plating. Thus they more easily penetrated the ship, causing considerable damage down below. The officer in command of the 15 cm. casemates was fortunately able to return the enemy fire, round for round. But the wireless cabin on the same deck was shattered and a Petty officer had his head blown off. Another shell which penetrated the after dressing station, and released the wounded there from their sufferings, killed the senior Staff Surgeon and the Squadron Chaplain.

The vessel's floating capability was now seriously impaired, for heavy shocks informed the control room faster than the voice pipes that we had been hit below the water-line by "short" enemy shells. The central stoke-hold filled so quickly that not all its occupants were able to reach the emergency exits. Another one soon met the same fate although the water entered more slowly. Even with all the pumps going, the ship's speed diminished, her draught increased and, despite flooding, we took a slight list to starboard.

About 3 p.m. the enemy made a fresh attempt to shift to us the unfavourable windward position and turned to port on an opposite course. If we had gone on, a circular action would have ensued, depriving us of the advantage of our position. Graf Spee therefore followed his movements and shortly afterwards swung round to starboard so that both lines were soon opposite to one another on a south-westerly course. This altered the objectives, the *Gneisenau* being opposed to the enemy's flagship, while the *Scharnhorst* now took on the second Battle Cruiser (*Inflexible*).

As we passed the *Scharnhorst* while swinging round, she also was already lying deeper in the water than usual and had a slight list to port. There was a large gaping hole forward and another on the quarter-deck. Funnels had fallen, smoke was pouring out, flames were visible inside the vessel through shot holes and scuttles. But her guns crashed out furiously and without intermission; the starboard side had just freshly joined in. Her fate, however, appeared to be sealed. She moved through the water ever more slowly and was suffering severely from the enemy's fire. At length the Commander-in-Chief seemed to feel that his flagship was nearing her end. As he had previously sacrificed the large cruisers for the lighter ones, so now he did the same with the *Scharnhorst* in her death-throes for the *Gneisenau*. In the firm determination to get as much out of her as possible as long as she remained afloat, and thus facilitate our escape, he turned to starboard towards the enemy, thinking that perhaps a torpedo might finish him off. What a hard decision, but what a magnificent one! the unquestioning faith which the whole group had always had in its Admiral, even when ignorant of his reasons and intentions, was now repaid a thousandfold by this sacrifice of himself. Again we passed the *Scharnhorst*. The water was already almost up to her forward outer decks. Fires were raging fore and aft, but the Admiral's flag flew proudly at the foremast, the Naval ensign at the mainmast. Gradually she heeled over to port, going down by the bow. When the forward turret was still about 6 ft. above water it fired its last round; then the propellers revolved in mid-air and the vessel sank rapidly, slanting forward, several thousand yards behind us. A huge cloud of steam and powder fumes, mixed with smoke and coal dust, rose up as high as our mast-head above her watery grave.

"The *Scharnhorst* waits for the *Gneisenau*" it seemed to say. A feeling of boundless loneliness, as of one who had lost his only friend and comrade in a deserted land, seized upon all who had witnessed her end. "Three points to starboard" the Captain commanded. He could not accept the Admiral's self-sacrificing offer as we had already suffered far too much ourselves. So he closed up to the enemy to reduce the distance between us.

We now had two Battle Cruisers opposed to us, and soon a third ship came clattering and barking upon the scene, an armoured cruiser of the Hampshire class, firing into our stern from 10 cm. guns as if the two of them were not enough. One of the big ships separated from her companion and made a large circle round us. One after another our starboard guns were put out of action. The armour of the after 15 cm. casemates was pierced and when the smoke cleared away the crew were found to be dead and the gun unusable. Another shell burst on the superstructure deck, hurling part of the crew of the forward 21 cm. gun into the forward 15 cm. casemate below; it cut a path for itself into the port 21 cm. casemate, and there also killed almost the whole crew simultaneously.

The ship's power of resistance was slowly waning, as I realized when making a tour of inspection down below. Piles of dead bodies and wreckage lay everywhere; in some places ice-cold water was trickling down, in others it was pouring in streams through hatches and shot-holes, extinguishing fires and soaking the men's clothes. Wherever there was any possibility of bringing a gun into action again the attempt was made. Reserves were brought up to replace the casualties, ammunition was carried up by hand where the lifts were no longer working. The action of the helm was disturbed by the fire of the enemy astern of us, and the *Gneisenau*, whose engines had been damaged and were only capable of slow speed, turned slowly to port. The ship was smothered in thick smoke which hid the view of the enemy's flagship. The others however were visible and we fired on them with our port guns as well as we could until they, too, were silenced. The after-turret had been put out of action some time ago, the forward one alone had not been hit and went on firing until its ammunition was exhausted. The latter was running short and it was a difficult and lengthy business to bring it up from the other guns amid the devastation. Hence the ship became quieter, for the enemy had also ceased to fire, doubtless supposing that we were done for. One final round flashed out angrily to port from the forward turret, the shell, as we were to learn later, penetrating far into the *Invincible's* hull. The enemy replied by re-opening fire, hitting the forward dressing station and tearing open the ship's side. Every round must strike home now for the hounds have run their quarry to earth, and are approaching warily to give it the death blow. The thunder gradually subsides, the bloody work is finished and it only

Extracts from "Graf Spee's Last Cruise"

remains for us to prevent the ship, which is still afloat, from falling into the enemy's hands and, if possible to save the survivors for the Fatherland. The men are ordered on deck and told to seize anything which will float. In perfect order they left their action stations, taking their wounded comrades with them. Ladders and gangways are almost non-existent, but in many places piles of iron wreckage afford a foothold by which to reach the deck. The bridge and Captain's cabin were intact, the helmsmen and sentries all at their posts awaiting further orders. One glance over the injured vessel's decks was sufficient to show how things had gone up there. The forward funnel was bent over to starboard, the other three showed holes, boils and great red patches where the grey paint had been chipped off. The main wireless had carried away, the tattered flag was jammed. The Naval Ensign at the fore had been shot away, but the black balls were still close under the yard, indicating "full speed ahead." Broken cordage dangled from the blocks, loose signal halliards blew about in the light breeze. Damaged guns of the light armament pointed upwards, while splinters lay around them. Through gaping holes in the deck and sides men were clambering out of the ship, black from the bunkers and stokehold, perspiring from the guns, all calm and orderly as if for roll call. Officers were standing in the battered boats, handing out wooden fittings and buoys; others were supervising the distribution of hammocks from the nettings. The men pressed forward, and as the ship slowly heeled over climbed to the port side, and thence scrambled down to the outer decks and prepared to go overboard. The British were closing in on us from three sides. Many a clenched fist was brandished and the men's fury found vent in full-blooded seamen's oaths. Then the Captain, who preserved his wonted calm to the last, ordered three cheers for H.M. the Emperor, and "Our good gallant *Gneisenau*" and proceeded to sink the ship. Our crew, who had really given their utmost in endurance and courage, complied with enthusiasm and the strains of "Deutschland über Alles" echoed through the ship with all its wonted vigour, followed by the hymn of the "Black, White and Red Flag" which was flying riddled with shot, at the mainmast-head and . . . .

At the "All hands overboard" the men slid or leapt over the edge into the water. The ship was listing more and more; I had to cling to the port end of the bridge to avoid sliding over to starboard. My faithful servant helped me out of my clothes. The *Gneisenau* quickly heeled over still further and began to capsize. I was fully conscious through what followed. I was now lying with my chest out on the railing and felt the ship sink from beneath me. The roaring and tossing of the water came ever nearer, and I concentrated my thoughts on the fact that it would be very cold before long. As the superstructure touched the water, the ship's speed in capsizing diminished and then she turned over further on her axis.

NAVAL & MERCANTILE HISTORY

Naval warfare is as old as conflict on land and as our title implies, maritime warfare is as important to us as terrestial battles. From the great galley battles of ancient Greece and Rome, Salamis and Actium, through the Barbary Coast pirates, the Spanish Armada and the long wars between England, France and Holland for control of colonial trade, control of the seas has meant political and economic power. Finally, with the sea battles of the Napoleonic Wars and the age of Nelson, maritime warfare entered the modern era. The two world wars saw the final end to Britain's domination of the seas and the emergence of the US as the maritime superpower.

The Naval and Military Press has a whole fleet of books covering the whole history of warfare at sea, just look and see!

THE LAST CRUISE OF THE "MAJESTIC"

Interesting personal account of the service of battleship "Majestic" in the Dardanelles arranged by Goodchild from the logbook of Petty Officer J.G. Cowie. "Majestic" was a Majestic-class pre-dreadnought battleship. In early 1915, she was dispatched to the Mediterranean for service in the Dardanelles Campaign. She participated in bombardments of Turkish forts and supported the Allied landings at Gallipoli. On 27 May 1915, she was torpedoed by the German submarine U-21 at Cape Helles, sinking with the loss of 49 men.

9781474539166

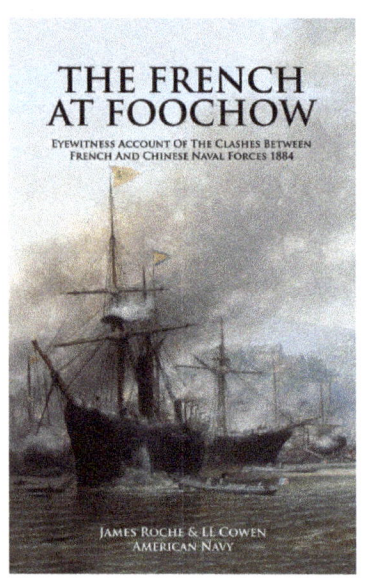

THE FRENCH AT FOOCHOW

Eyewitness Account Of The Clashes Between French And Chinese Naval Forces 1884

Eyewitness account by two American Navy officers of the clashes between French and Chinese naval forces following the collapse of the Li-Fournier Agreement. Two tables show detail of each side's ships and their specifications, as well as the damage they sustained.

9781474540766

"SEVERN'S" SAGA

Keble Chatterton turns his attention to the history of HMS Severn, a British monitor that duelled with the Konigsberg in the Rufijiand and also took part in the attack on Tanga and other operations in East Africa until the end of the war. Based on interviews with many of the protagonists and original manuscripts, both British and German, this is the story of a ship whose five-year career was packed tight with action from start to finish.

9781474537001

LOW`S HISTORY of the INDIAN NAVY

This is an extremely rare work, in its original edition, and covers the life span of the Indian Navy, 1600 to 1863. Operations from the Persian Gulf to the Burma and First China Wars, from Aden to New Zealand and the Maori Wars, and the Indian Mutiny. Survey work from the Red Sea to the China Seas.

9781474536530

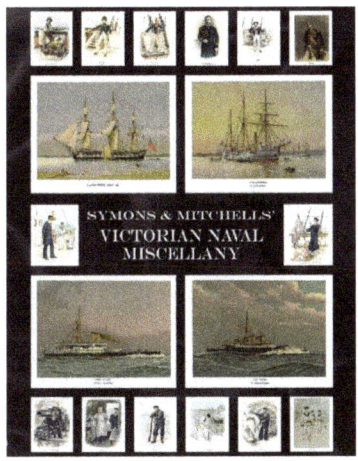

SYMONS & MITCHELLS' VICTORIAN NAVAL MISCELLANY

Sailors' Costumes & Ships Of The British fleet In Colour

A beautifully illustrated snapshot of British Navy uniforms, Actions & Ships produced at the later part of the Queen Victoria's reign. An absolute must for anyone with an interest in the dress, and history of the Royal Navy.

9781474536349

DARDANELLES DILEMMA

The Story of the Naval Operations

In his vivid writing style, Keble Chatterton gives a full and well-illustrated history of a naval operation that was plagued by inept planning and command. A valuable source for those interested in the naval and seafaring aspect of the attempt to knock Germany's ally, Turkey, out of World War I, originally published in 1935, this is an authentic account that uses Official records with officers' spoken accounts and their personal diaries. These give the modern reader a detailed picture, impossible to gather today, due to the passage of time that places it no longer within living memory.

9781474537018

THE FIGHTING AT JUTLAND

The Personal Experiences of Sixty Officers and Men of the British Fleet

An extremely useful tool for those studying the events at Jutland in 1916, this was the first major action between two enemy fleets since the Battle of Trafalgar. This is a faithful reproduction of the compilers' original privately published edition, that was abbreviated for later commercial editions, none of these later editions were as complete or attractive as this.

Lt. Comm Fawcet & Lt Hooper wanted to give the British public a better idea of exactly what went on during the Battle. These two diligent Naval Officers - who had also been present at the Battle, collected together accounts from those who had fought in British ships, to give the British public a better idea of exactly what went on during the Battle.

9781474537025

naval-military-press.com

www.ingramcontent.com/pod-product-compliance
Lightning Source LLC
Chambersburg PA
CBHW060925170426
43192CB00024B/2896